STERLING BIOGRAPHIES

Matthew Henson

The Quest for the North Pole

D0465384

Kathleen Olmstead

STERLING

New York / London
www.sterlingpublishing.com/kids

To everyone who risked the great unknown . . .

STERLING and the distinctive Sterling logo are registered trademarks of
Sterling Publishing Co., Inc.

Library of Congress Cataloging-in-Publication Data
Olmstead, Kathleen.
Matthew Henson: the quest for the North Pole/Kathleen Olmstead.
p.cm.-- (Sterling biographies)
Includes bibliographical references and index.
ISBN-13: 978-1-4027-4441-9
1. Henson, Matthew Alexander, 1866-1955-- Juvenile literature. 2. Explorers -- United States--
Biography-- Juvenile literature. 3. African American explorers-- Biography--Juvenile literature. 4.
North Pole--Discovery and exploration--Juvenile literature. I. Title.

G635.H4046 2008
910.9163'2--dc22   2007048106

10 9 8 7 6 5 4 3 2 1

Published by Sterling Publishing Co., Inc.
387 Park Avenue South, New York, NY 10016

Distributed in Canada by Sterling Publishing
c/o Canadian Manda Group, 165 Dufferin Street
Toronto, Ontario, Canada M6K 3H6
Distributed in the United Kingdom by GMC Distribution Services
Castle Place, 166 High Street, Lewes, East Sussex, England BN7 1XU
Distributed in Australia by Capricorn Link (Australia) Pty. Ltd.
P.O. Box 704, Windsor, NSW 2756, Australia

Printed in China

Sterling ISBN 978-1-4027-4441-9 (paperback)

Sterling ISBN 978-1-4027-6060-0 (hardcover)

For information about custom editions, special sales, premium and
corporate purchases, please contact Sterling Special Sales
Department at 800-805-5489 or specialsales@sterlingpublishing.com.

Designed by Erica Kalish for SimonSays Design!
Image research by Larry Schwartz

Contents

Events in the Life of Matthew Henson

1866

August 8, 1866
Matthew Alexander Henson is born in Charles County, Maryland, the third of six children.

1879–1884
Henson travels the world; Captain Childs teaches him to read.

November 1887–Spring 1888
Henson departs with Robert E. Peary for Nicaragua and works as Peary's assistant while Peary surveys for a canal.

April 16, 1891
Henson marries Eva Flint of Philadelphia; immediately leaves in June for the North Greenland Expedition. They live with Inuit for more than a year.

September 1895
Henson returns from the North and finds work at the American Museum of Natural History in New York. The Peary expedition delivers two meteorites found at Cape York, Greenland.

July 1898
Henson returns to Greenland with Peary. The expedition lasts four years. They arrive at the northern coast of Greenland.

July 1905
Henson and Peary take the *Roosevelt* to Cape Sheridan on Ellesmere Island. They reach the farthest north before returning on December 24, 1906.

July 6, 1908
Henson leaves with Peary for the North on the *Roosevelt*; the expedition lands at Cape Sheridan in September.

April 6, 1909
Henson, Peary, and four Inuit companions arrive at the North Pole.

1913
Henson begins work as a messenger at the U.S. Customs House in New York City. He remains there until his retirement in 1936.

1944
Henson receives the Peary Polar Medal from the U.S. Congress. The medal is given to all living members of the 1909 expedition team.

1954
Matthew and Lucy Henson visit the White House and President Eisenhower to commemorate Henson's trip to the North Pole.

1877
At age 11, Henson runs away to Washington, D.C., and gets a job in a restaurant; later, walks to Baltimore and finds work as a cabin boy.

1884–1887
After the death of Captain Childs, Henson returns to America to look for work; eventually finds a job at a hat store in Washington, D.C.

Spring 1889
Henson moves to Philadelphia and finds work at the League Island Navy Yard.

June 1893
Henson goes north again. Plagued with bad weather, the journey is abandoned. Henson and Peary remain north another year.

Summer 1897
Henson and Peary return with the third, and largest, meteorite from Cape York; Henson and Eva decide to divorce.

1902
Henson works as a porter for the Pullman Railcar Company.

September 1907
Matthew Henson marries Lucy Jane Ross.

1909
Henson sets out on a lecture tour. Ticket sales are slow, Henson is a nervous speaker, and the remaining part of tour is cancelled.

1912
A Negro Explorer at the North Pole is published. Henson hopes royalties from the book will support him and his wife, but sales are poor.

1937
Henson is at last allowed membership into the Explorers Club.

1947
Bradley Robinson collaborates with Henson to write *Dark Companion*. The book is a success and more people are interested in Henson's story.

March 9, 1955
Matthew Henson dies in New York. In 1988, his body is moved to Arlington National Cemetery near the grave of Robert Peary.

1955

To Reach the North Pole

Henson must go with me. I cannot make it without him.

—Robert E. Peary

They had been on the ice for weeks. His body was exhausted but he wouldn't slow down. Matthew Henson's dog team struggled to pull his sled over the rough and jagged ice. He dug in one foot then braced himself to push off, trying to lift the sled at the same time. It would be easier to grip the handles if he removed his seal skin mitts, but Henson knew that the frigid temperature—almost sixty degrees below zero—would quickly freeze his skin. Up ahead, he could see Lieutenant Peary with his sled.

Suddenly he felt the ground shift, and the sheet of ice that they were crossing abruptly disappeared beneath him. Henson dropped into the freezing water of the Polar Sea.

Was this how it would end? After years of trying to reach the North Pole, would his quest end beneath the ice? Then, just as suddenly, a hand took hold of his jacket and he was lifted to safety. Henson gasped for air and opened his eyes. He was still alive and just as determined. His quest would continue and this time—despite his humble beginnings—he would succeed and become one of the most celebrated explorers of the twentieth century.

CHAPTER 1

Henson's Story Begins

*Your fight is with the ignorance in people's minds,
and your best weapons are knowledge and intelligence.
These books are the beginning. Make them your
fists, Matthew.*

—*Captain Childs*, Dark Companion

It was the end of the **Civil War**, and life in America, especially for African Americans, was changing quickly. For former slaves, it was the start to a life of freedom. Men, women, and children could no longer be owned by another person. Although they still faced racial intolerance from many people, African Americans could travel and work with much more freedom. They were looking for work and new homes after years of hardship and oppression under the system of slavery.

However, unlike many of the just-freed slaves, the Lemuel Henson family was already free and were sharecroppers in Charles County, Maryland, where Lemuel, his wife, and their two children worked on a farm near the Potomac River, about forty-four miles south of Washington, D.C. They did not own their land. As sharecroppers, they worked the fields for a landlord and rented a small house on the farm. Rather than paying them wages, the landlord took a large portion of the Henson's crops. It was very hard work and they were often left with little food for themselves after harvest.

A freed slave uses a plow, much like Lemuel Henson did, while working the fields as a sharecropper. This illustration is dated 1866—the same year that Matthew was born.

An Unhappy Childhood

On August 8, 1866, the Hensons welcomed their third child into the world—Matthew Alexander Henson. According to *Dark Companion*, a biography of Henson published late in his life, his mother died when he was two years old and his father quickly remarried. Although Lemuel had a bad temper, he could also be kind to his children. However, Matthew's stepmother Nellie was often cruel. She beat the children and forced them to work long hours in the fields. There was no time for school and little time for games.

When Matthew was about seven, he suffered another great loss. His father suddenly died from injuries while pushing a cart. Now there were six Henson children, and Matthew and his five siblings were left alone with Nellie.

Life with his stepmother continued to be horrendous. The beatings became more frequent, and after several years, the farm fell into ruin. One day, as the story is told in *Dark Companion*, Matthew accidentally spilled a bucket of water on the kitchen floor. Nellie

Different Versions of Henson's Life

An illustration made from a photograph of Henson in his arctic outfit.

It is hard to verify stories from Henson's childhood. There are no school records, letters, or stories from other family members to confirm or deny details. This wouldn't normally be a problem except that in two separate biographies and several interviews, Henson seemed to arbitrarily change some of the details of his life story.

In his first book, *A Negro Explorer at the North Pole*, Henson claims his family moved to Washington when he was seven years old. When his mother died, he was raised by an uncle and had six years of schooling before running away to Baltimore. In *Dark Companion*, published thirty-five years later, Henson says his family remained on the farm where he was born. His mother died when he was two years old and his father when he was seven, and an abusive stepmother raised him. This book was written in collaboration with writer Bradley Robinson, who might have exaggerated some of the story for dramatic effect. Although most sources say Henson started working as a cabin boy at the age of eleven, others state that he was thirteen when he went to sea.

He continued to tell different versions throughout his life, even changing details about his adventures in the Arctic. It's hard to say if Henson felt more comfortable telling the truth as the years passed or if he simply chose to tell a more dramatic story.

An 1865 photograph depicts the Washington, D.C., streets that Henson likely roamed after running away from home as a boy.

beat him so badly that he spent three days in bed. Even though he was only eleven years old, Matthew decided to run away.

In the middle of the night, after everyone else was asleep, Matthew crawled out of bed. Using torn pieces of blanket, he wrapped both his feet very carefully. He moved very slowly through the house, the blankets muffling the sounds of his footsteps. He closed the door quietly behind him and walked toward the road. He took nothing with him. There was nothing special he owned that he wanted to keep.

Running Away to a New Life

Matthew walked all the way—all forty-four miles—to Washington, D.C. He was cold and hungry and scared, but he knew that he needed to find work and shelter. Luckily, it didn't take him long. Again, according to a story in *Dark Companion*, he found a job in a restaurant called Janey's Home-Cooked Meals Café. It was owned by a kind-hearted woman named Janey Moore—but everyone called her Aunt Janey. Although she had never met Matthew before, she welcomed the young boy like he was a long-lost relative. For the first time in a long time, Matthew felt safe and at home.

He worked as a dishwasher and became a waiter after a few months. Matthew liked talking to the customers and listening to all their stories. One customer in particular—Baltimore Jack—enthralled Matthew. Jack was a sailor. He claimed to own his own ship and told Matthew about all his adventures at sea. Jack had traveled around the world, faced terrible storms, fought off bandits, and made it all the way back to Aunt Janey's restaurant to entertain Matthew with his stories. The young boy needed no further convincing. He wanted a life at sea, too.

As a young boy, Matthew wanted a life on the sea—possibly on a clipper ship like the one shown in this 1875 Currier & Ives lithograph. Clippers were narrow ships with large sails. They were fast and often sailed sea trade routes.

Aunt Janey tried to persuade Matthew that Jack's stories were simply tall tales. She insisted that no one would let a black man be in charge of his own ship, but Matthew wouldn't listen. Aunt Janey knew there was nothing more she could say. Matthew would have to learn about **prejudice** on his own. He was a nice boy and a good worker and she was sad to see him go.

Matthew left a few days later carrying a package of food and one dollar from Aunt Janey. Once again, he had a long walk ahead of him. It was sixty miles to Baltimore, Maryland, and he didn't want to waste a moment in starting his new life.

Life at Sea

Matthew quickly found work on the *Katie Hines*, the first ship he approached when he arrived in Baltimore. The boat's captain was named Captain Childs. Although Matthew had spent very little time with white men, he saw something special in Captain Childs and knew he could trust this white-haired man. Childs certainly noticed Matthew. He saw a small, scruffy boy who needed a good meal and a place to sleep. When Matthew said he wanted to work on a ship, the captain took a chance on him. This would prove to be a fateful and hopeful decision for both.

When Matthew said he wanted to work on a ship, the captain took a chance on him.

Matthew was happy on board the *Katie Hines*. His life at sea, between 1879 and 1884, was nothing like what Baltimore Jack described, but he did see the world, including China, Japan, the Philippines, North Africa, Spain, and Russia. Although most of his time was spent performing his cabin-boy duties—keeping the captain's quarters clean, running errands, helping out in the kitchen—Matthew always lent a hand to others on board whenever possible, to learn as much as he could. And learn he did. Matthew became such a good carpenter that he could build or fix anything on the ship. He also trained as a medic, so he could assist with first aid whenever someone was sick or hurt.

Captain Childs encouraged Matthew to ask questions. The captain believed that curiosity was an important part of learning. He taught Matthew that exploring with his mind was as important as seeing the world. To understand the world, Captain Childs told Matthew, he should understand history and read literature. Childs took on the task of teaching Matthew how to read and write.

Learning to Read

Almost every night, after all his work was done, Matthew sat down with books and a candle. Childs didn't have to work long with him before Matthew was reading on his own. In his later years, Henson happily recalled his evenings with history books and adventure stories. He soon saw that Captain Childs was right. Even though he was seeing so much of the world first hand, he was learning a great deal more inside books.

Although Henson maintained that Captain Childs taught him well, there is some doubt as to whether Henson could read and write at the level he claimed. There are very few examples of Henson's handwriting in existence even though he is said to have kept a diary. Robert Bryce, who has written a great deal about the quest to reach the North Pole, suspects that Henson could only read and write slightly. Bryce thinks that Henson dictated his letters, only providing his signature at the bottom.

Meeting Prejudice Along the Way

Not all of Henson's life on the *Katie Hines* was ideal. There were crew members that called him names because of the color of his skin. He also faced **racism** whenever he left the ship. While stopping at ports around the world, he encountered ridicule and acts of **segregation**. Because he experienced freedom and kindness from the captain, the hurt from these acts felt even crueler to Henson.

There were crew members that called him names because of the color of his skin.

In *Dark Companion*, Henson describes feeling angry and wanting to lash out, but Childs offers him an important piece of advice.

"Your life is not going to be easy, Matthew, and it'll be harder if you try to beat your way through with your fists," he said. Matthew tried to protest but the captain cut him off. "Your fight is with the ignorance in people's minds, and your best weapons are knowledge and intelligence."

Later that night, Matthew lay in his bunk and thought about the captain's words. He was especially moved by Childs's parting thought. The captain picked up a history book that was on the table. He held it in front of him and said, "These books are the beginning. Make them your fists, Matthew."

This scene may not have happened exactly as described but Henson clearly wanted to get an important message across. Learning to read and write—getting an education—was his best defense against ignorance and racism.

Life After the Sea

When Henson was eighteen years old, as the ship was returning from Jamaica, Captain Childs became very ill. Despite all of Henson's efforts and prayers, Captain Childs died in 1884.

This was another huge blow to the young man. Childs was like a father to him. He had always believed in Henson and had given him every chance to learn. Unlike most white men—certainly anyone that Henson had met in his young life—Childs did not treat him as a lesser person because of his color. Henson knew he was lucky to have met Childs and wondered if he would find anyone like him again.

Unlike most white men—certainly anyone that Henson had met in his young life—Childs did not treat him as a lesser person because of his color.

Henson left the *Katie Hines* and found work on another boat called the *White Seal*. He was not happy, though. His new captain was verbally abusive and often drunk. The crew and ship were dirty and he faced racial slurs and insults daily. Henson soon realized this was not the life for him. When the ship docked in St. John's, Newfoundland, Henson left. He booked passage on another ship for Boston and headed back to America.

He tried a few different jobs, moving from city to city, but found nothing suitable. Feeling at a loss, Henson returned to Washington, D.C., the only home he had known.

In 1887, he was working at Steinmetz and Sons, a local hat store. It was an ordinary job—his days spent in the stockroom— but the work was steady and the owners were nice. Henson expected his life would be quiet and unexciting for quite some time. Little did he know that this job would change his life!

CHAPTER 2

New Adventure in Nicaragua

It is well known that the chief characteristic of Commander Peary is persistency which, coupled with fortitude, is the secret of his success.

Matthew Henson was hard at work as usual. His job at Steinmetz and Sons was certainly easier than his life at sea, but there was still plenty to keep him occupied. Henson liked to always be busy. He knew Captain Childs would have expected no less.

One afternoon, Mr. Steinmetz called Henson to the front of the store. He introduced Henson to Lieutenant Robert E. Peary, a tall man with red hair and a large moustache. Mr. Steinmetz explained that Peary was going to Nicaragua in Central America and needed a personal assistant. The lieutenant wanted someone with a lot of experience at sea, and Mr. Steinmetz was recommending Henson for the job.

Henson liked Lieutenant Peary right away. The lieutenant was not overly friendly—being rather gruff, in fact—but he had a firm handshake and looked Henson in the eye when he spoke.

An undated photo of Robert E. Peary depicts a man of comfortable means. Unlike Henson, Peary lived a pleasant life with his widowed mother, attending high school and then college before joining the navy.

Many people did not show him this respect because of the color of his skin. Henson thought Peary might be different.

Peary explained that as an engineer, the U.S. Navy was sending him to Nicaragua to **survey** its land. The American government wanted to dig a canal across Nicaragua that would connect the Atlantic and Pacific Oceans. Nicaragua and Panama were both possibilities. It was Peary's job to determine which would provide the best route. The project required cutting through jungles in extremely hot weather. Peary wanted to prepare Henson for the hard work ahead. The job would be nothing like working in a hat store!

Henson, realizing the lieutenant didn't know how hard he worked on the *Katie Hines*, assured Peary that he was ready, willing, and able.

In the Jungles of Nicaragua

They left New York Harbor in November 1887 on the steamer ship *Hondo*, and Henson fell back into his ship routine in no time at all. After ensuring that Lieutenant Peary was comfortable and needed nothing more each day, Henson helped on deck. He worked happily while waiting for his chance to start a new adventure. The steamer arrived in Jamaica a week later. The country was beautiful—lush green trees and mountain tops, clear blue waters. However, their stay in Jamaica was very short. Peary only needed to hire men for his crew, and in no time at all, they had a hundred men plus three cooks. They were all ready to head into the jungles of Nicaragua for months of hard work.

He worked happily while waiting for his chance to start a new adventure.

For the most part, Henson's new job as "manservant" for Lieutenant Peary was very similar to working with Captain Childs. Whatever job needed to be done, he was right there to do it. Henson stayed at the camp—a group of tents, fire pits, and wooden lean-tos set up in a clearing—while the others went farther into the jungle. It was difficult being so far removed from the action, but Henson did not take his work lightly. He was there to ensure Peary had clean clothes and a comfortable life while in Nicaragua.

Henson cooked, cleaned, and mended clothes when necessary. He built the wooden lean-tos as shelters and helped others around camp. He even used his skills as a medic when someone was hurt. It was not long before everyone relied on Henson in some way or another.

Then, one day, a worker in the jungle was hurt. Peary, already impressed by Henson's work ethic and skills around camp, asked Henson if he could help in the jungle instead.

A c. 1890 photograph shows work being done on the Nicaraguan canal with logs being used to make a path along the trail.

Henson said yes right away. The workers were cutting down trees and pulling up stumps—hard, backbreaking labor in the jungle heat. Henson worked the long hours alongside them without complaint. He no longer felt he was only a servant and quickly proved to Peary that he had more to offer. He worked with the crew in the jungle but still managed to help Peary with his day-to-day activities.

It was not long before everyone relied on Henson in some way or another.

The lieutenant wasn't too surprised. Henson, he thought, might be slender, and looked rather young for his age, but he held a lot of promise. Henson and Peary left the jungles of Nicaragua after seven months, returning to Washington in the spring of 1888. Peary returned to his naval duties in Philadelphia, while Henson went back to his old job in the stockroom at Steinmetz and Sons. Ultimately, the Nicaraguan canal was never built. Instead, the Panama Canal became the designated site and was opened in 1914.

Plans for an Expedition to Greenland

While in Nicaragua, Peary was already thinking about a new adventure. He wanted to lead an expedition through Greenland—the world's largest island. It was situated in the northern Atlantic Ocean and Polar Sea, and two-thirds of the island was covered with ice.

He had been there once before—in 1886—during a leave from the navy. Although he didn't mention it to many people, Peary had a grand goal in mind. He wanted to be the first man to reach the North Pole. An expedition through Greenland would provide the opportunity to plan a route. He needed to find the best way to get to the top of the world—and to international fame.

Peary was certain Henson would make a perfect addition to his team, so he spoke to Henson about his plans for Greenland. Henson listened to the lieutenant's description of a land of ice and snow and endless white. It was the opposite of their days in Nicaragua, and Henson was very excited. It sounded so beautiful.

Peary made two things clear. First of all, he definitely wanted Henson to come with him. The second point, unfortunately, was that Peary couldn't pay him. It would not be a navy trip, so Peary had to raise money on his own. Henson said there was no need to worry. He recognized a wonderful opportunity when he heard it. Henson was willing to go without pay.

This is an aerial photograph of Greenland showing the land that Peary hoped to explore with Henson.

Robert Edwin Peary (1856–1920)

Robert Peary is credited with being the first man to reach the North Pole. Born in Pennsylvania, he studied at Bowdoin College in Maine and graduated with a civil engineering degree. When he was twenty-five years old, he was commissioned in the U.S. Navy as a lieutenant.

A portrait of Peary c. 1909 photographed shortly after returning from the North Pole.

Peary was sent on a variety of navy assignments throughout America and Central America to survey and map the land. It is, however, for his life as an explorer that he is remembered. He was a very driven and ambitious man, who would let nothing, and no one, slow him down. He led more than a half dozen expeditions into the Arctic in his quest to be the first man at the North Pole.

Peary married Josephine Diebitsch in 1888, and they had two children. He wrote several books about his arctic adventures and trips to the North Pole and was appointed as a rear admiral in the navy in 1911 in recognition for his work in the Arctic. Robert Peary died on February 20, 1920, and was buried in Arlington Cemetery in Washington, D.C.

Waiting to Start a New Adventure

The lieutenant wanted everything in place and ready to go as soon as funding for the expedition was found. That also meant he wanted Henson close by. Peary promised Henson that he would send for him as soon as he could. Henson waited. When word finally arrived that Peary found him a job as messenger at the League Island Navy Yard, Henson quickly packed his bags and left for Philadelphia in the spring of 1889.

However, the long wait continued in Philadelphia. While Peary searched for financial backing for his trip, Henson settled into his new life in Philadelphia—a bustling city with a large African American community. It didn't take Henson long to meet new friends—and one special person in particular.

Shortly after arriving in the city, Henson joined a new church. It was there that he met Eva Flint. She was a year younger than Henson. On April 16, 1891, Matthew Henson and Eva Flint were married.

Word finally came that the departure date for Greenland was set for June 1891. Henson faced a serious setback, though. The navy wouldn't grant him a leave of absence from his job. If Henson decided to go with Peary then he would have to quit his navy job and all the security that it offered.

His wife didn't want him to go north with Peary. She was worried that he wouldn't come back or that he wouldn't have a job when he did return. For Henson, though, the answer was quite simple: He would go with Peary. There were no guarantees that the expedition would meet its goals, but he had faith in his own abilities and the lieutenant's leadership. Also, Henson believed that whatever might happen, as long as he was loyal and hardworking, Peary would always take care of him.

CHAPTER 3

The North Greenland Expedition

Naturally the impressions formed on my first visit to the Land of Ice and Snow were the most lasting, but . . . I was to learn . . . that such a life was no picnic, and to realize what primitive life meant.

It was June 6, 1891, as Matthew Henson watched the dock from the rail of the *Kite*. He had set sail many times before but never with a crowd this size seeing him off. Lieutenant Peary was leaving for a year in the Arctic, and it seemed everyone was excited about it. They cheered and waved as the ship pulled away from the harbor in Brooklyn, New York.

Peary's original goal for the expedition was to be the first to cross Greenland (east to west) by sled. Unfortunately, Fridtjof Nansen, a Norwegian explorer, beat him to it in 1888. As a result, Peary decided to go north instead. A great deal of Greenland was still unexplored.

A great deal of Greenland was still unexplored. . . . [and] no one knew how far north the land stretched.

Although local people known as Inuit had lived there for centuries and Europeans had many settlements, no one knew how far north the land stretched. By mapping this unknown territory, Peary hoped he might also find the best route to the

This c. 1910 photograph shows three Inuit people preparing to leave on a hunt. The children are sitting in a kayak, an Inuit boat similar to a canoe.

North Pole. Perhaps he would even find a strip of land that led directly to the top of the world!

Henson liked seeing his name in print even if the newspaper stories were not always kind. There was much debate about whether it was wise to take a black man to the Arctic. Unfortunately, during Henson's lifetime, some people and newspapers expressed their racist and misguided opinions without a second thought. People wondered if someone of Henson's race could survive in the extreme cold. Some people thought African Americans were better suited for hot climates. Henson knew that this was yet another example of some

The North Pole

This picture shows close up of a compass face with needles pointing north and south.

When you hold a compass, the needle always points north, which is magnetic north, and is not a fixed point on Earth. It doesn't indicate an actual place—just the direction north.

Geographic north can be found at the northern tip of Earth's **axis**. It is located in the middle of the Arctic Ocean, so any explorer must travel on ice over the Polar Sea to reach it. Whenever people mention the North Pole—including Henson and Peary—they are usually referring to geographic north.

From January to June, the North Pole can have daylight that lengthens to almost twenty-four hours a day. From July to December, it can have darkness that lengthens to almost twenty-four hours a day. This is determined by Earth's rotation and whether the Sun is north of the **equator** or south of it. However, it is almost never dark, or light, for twenty-four hours straight. Even on the shortest days of the year, there is a thin line of twilight along the horizon for a brief time.

people's ignorance, and he quite wisely did his best to brush it aside. They also questioned Lieutenant Peary's decision to bring his wife Josephine along. According to some reporters, it was complete folly to bring a black man and a woman on an arctic exploration!

Henson found many jobs to occupy his time on the *Kite*. As Peary's assistant, he was always on duty, always ready to help the lieutenant whenever asked. Henson had more experience at sea then the other team members, including Peary. He pitched in wherever he was needed, organized supplies, and started to build the sleds for their journey across the snow.

Mrs. Josephine Peary, pictured here with her husband, Robert, accompanied him on several arctic journeys and wrote books about her adventures.

Peary's Chosen Crew

This staged photograph of Dr. Cook in his arctic outfit was taken c. 1911. At the time, Cook was a famous explorer in his own right.

Almost all of Peary's crew for his 1891 expedition was carefully chosen for their specific skills. He knew Matthew Henson from his trip to Nicaragua and knew Henson was a good assistant in the field. Eivind Astrup, a student from Norway, had experience with ice and northern climates. Peary brought Frederick A. Cook along as the ship's surgeon. Although it was the first trip north for Dr. Cook, Peary instinctively felt Cook would be a good addition to the team. Langdon Gibson, an ornithologist, was included, so he could conduct research on birds and wildlife found in the area.

Only John Verhoeff was chosen for another reason: Peary was in need of further financing for the expedition, and Verhoeff offered $2,000 to come along as a mineralogist. Peary agreed as long as Verhoeff didn't expect special treatment. The young man accepted the terms and joined Peary's team.

Traveling to McCormick Bay

On June 30, they arrived in Disko Bay on the west coast of Greenland. It was nothing like Henson imagined. He was expecting an icy wonderland with snowy peaks on mountain tops, but springtime in Greenland was full of color. Henson looked over the clear waters of the bay to a landscape of green hills and wildflowers. He was surprised by its majestic and colorful beauty.

After a few days rest, the *Kite* continued on its northward journey. Ice was still a serious concern even during the warmer months. There were large sheets of ice—known as floes—that would break off glaciers or icebergs and float through the water. If a ship became trapped between floes, it could be crushed as the floes crashed into each other. The ship sailed into Baffin Bay while staying close to the coastline. There would be fewer ice floes closer to shore where the water was slightly warmer.

The *Kite* had almost reached its destination in McCormick Bay when it was caught in a sea of ice. Now, this was the scene that Henson expected in the north! Moving forward was very

A modern day photograph shows a bird's eye view of Disko Bay, Greenland, where the *Kite* landed in June 1891.

This modern photograph shows a boat stuck in the ice in Disko Bay, Greenland. As sheets of ice move over the sea, they can easily crush a trapped boat. This was always a great danger for the *Kite* and her crew.

slow going indeed, and often the *Kite* couldn't move in any direction. While the ship's captain and his crew worked to break free of the ice, Peary stood on deck watching the action.

Suddenly, the *Kite* shifted. It was a quick, violent movement and Peary was thrown across the deck, breaking his leg. Dr. Cook, the expedition's surgeon, set the bone and ordered bed rest. Peary returned to his cabin where he remained for the next few weeks. He hated to miss all the excitement on deck but knew his leg must be strong for his long trek in the new year.

Meeting the Inuit

It was July 26 when the *Kite* finally made it through the ice and landed on the shore of McCormick Bay. Peary was carried to land on a stretcher while supplies were unloaded. Wood, fuel, canned goods, and personal items were stacked along the rocky shore. Despite the ice in the bay, there was no snow on land. There was plenty of mud, moss, and green grass over the shore and hills. A large cliff sheltering the beach was covered in **red lichen**. Peary ordered the men to build their winter shelter beneath the red cliff.

They were not alone, though. The Inuit of the region greeted Peary's men and the crew of the *Kite*. Explorers and hunters, both European and American, had been visiting Greenland for many years. As a colony of Denmark, many nonnative people lived or worked there, so the Inuit were not surprised when the *Kite* arrived.

They assumed they would meet a group of men with goods to trade. When they saw Henson, however, they knew things would be different. The Inuit had never seen a black man before, and they were amazed. They pushed Henson's coat sleeve up so they could look at his skin—it was dark just like theirs. He was welcomed as a brother. They thought he was an Inuit from the south, and Henson didn't correct them.

This undated photograph shows Peary trading goods with an Inuit. He also brought home many Inuit items and sold them to museums and private collectors.

Inuit vs. Eskimo

The Inuit people of the northern regions—mainly Alaska, Greenland, and Canada's north—call themselves *Inuit*, which means "the people." Also known as *Eskimo*, which translates to "eater of raw flesh" in the Algonquin language, most Inuit consider the name Eskimo offensive. It was misapplied until only recently, which is why direct quotations from Henson or Peary in this book still contain the word.

Due to their remote locations, many Inuit communities continued to live with little outside influence until the 1950s or 1960s. There was not much change since the days when Henson and Peary lived with them. Today, most Inuit live with electricity, technology, and the extra conveniences of modern life. These changes have also meant a loss of Inuit language and some of their traditional culture

The Inuit of present-day Greenland live in houses but try to keep their unique culture alive. Here, two Inuit girls wear traditional clothes in front of modern homes.

Red Cliff House

Upon arriving at McCormick Bay, Henson and the others needed to move quickly before winter arrived. In Greenland, snowstorms could appear as early as August. The *Kite* had to return home, and the ice was already causing problems. It would only get worse as the weather grew colder.

Because Henson had the most carpentry experience, he took charge of the shelter construction and ended up doing most of the work. Everyone slept in tents along the shore or in cabins back on the ship while they worked. They finished Red Cliff House, named after the lichen on the cliff above it, by the beginning of August. The *Kite* sailed days later leaving Peary, Henson, Mrs. Peary, and the four-man crew at McCormick Bay.

Red Cliff House was not a simple shack by the side of a cliff. Although it was small— twenty-two feet long, twelve feet wide, and eight feet high—they tried to make it as comfortable as possible. The house was divided into two rooms: the larger one for the crew and the smaller one for the Pearys. Rugs covered the walls for extra insulation. They furnished the rooms with beds, tables, books, and photographs from home. Mrs. Peary decorated her space with extra curtains and carpets. A black round stove sat in the middle of each room to keep them warm. A long pipe went from the stove to a hole in the ceiling to let all the smoke out. They covered the outside of the house with tarpaper and built a stone wall about four feet away. All their supplies were stored between the wall and Red Cliff House.

Because Henson had the most carpentry experience, he took charge of the shelter construction and ended up doing most of the work.

Both rooms in Red Cliff House had a stove much like the one pictured in this photograph. They were the only sources of heat over the long winter.

The crew finished the construction just in time to celebrate Henson's birthday. Lieutenant Peary and his wife hosted a special meal in his honor. Everyone sat in the larger room that also doubled as a living room and enjoyed a meal of duck breast. This was a new experience for Henson. As he later commented, "Never before in my life had the anniversary of my birth been celebrated, and to have a party given in my honor touched me deeply."

Winter Preparations Begin

Henson, the Pearys, and the rest of the crew were going to spend at least a year in Greenland, and most had no idea what to expect. They were all anxious to start on the trek northward, but they couldn't begin until the following spring. If they left in the fall, when the days were getting shorter, they would be traveling in near total darkness. They needed to wait until there was enough daylight to find their way. The men also needed time to adapt to their new environment and learn possibly life-saving skills from the Inuit.

With Henson's help, Peary began to trade guns, needles, and tin plates with the Inuit people for furs, extra clothing, and dogs for their sled teams. Inuit women were hired to sew outfits for all the men and Mrs. Peary. These loose outfits were made out of animal skins—usually fox, wolf, or polar bear—and would keep them as dry and as warm as possible. Although the clothing was bulky, members of the expedition could still move easily while wearing them. The jackets, or parkas, had large hoods with fur trim to protect them from the wind and snow.

Boots, known as *kamiks*, and hats were made from sealskin or caribou skin, which also kept the body warm and dry. When traveling over snow, the Inuit wore **snowshoes**, which prevented them from sinking down into the deep snow. The lieutenant knew they could trade for these goods once they arrived in Greenland, so he used space on the *Kite* for extra fuel, alcohol for their stoves, and canned supplies with which to trade.

This c. 1910 photograph shows Henson in his hooded fur parka. Any ice on the fur could be broken off, stopping the parka from becoming soaking wet and freezing solid like a wool parka would have done.

Learning from the Inuit

In order to learn from the Inuit, Henson needed to understand them. When he worked on the *Katie Hines*, Henson found that he could pick up languages easily. While others on Peary's team would only pick up a few words, Henson learned to speak the Inuit language fluently. Henson, therefore, also took on the job of interpreter. Lieutenant Peary relied on him to communicate all their needs to the Inuit, and as the Inuit grew to consider Henson family, it became hard for them to say no to his requests.

Whenever he wasn't busy building sleds and helping Peary, Henson was working with the Inuit. He joined his new friends on hunting and fishing trips. Among other things, they showed him how to track a herd of musk oxen—a small type of ox found in northern Canada and Greenland.

He also joined in while hunting polar bears, hares, seals, and walruses. The Inuit used the rifles that Peary brought, but there had been a time when they killed their prey with harpoons and spears made from bone.

Henson watched as they skinned and butchered the dead animals. He observed that the Inuit did not discard any part of

A 19th-century line engraving shows an Inuit in a kayak, using a harpoon to kill a narwhal, a type of Arctic whale.

Even in modern times, as shown in this photograph from 1993, the Inuit use traditional methods of skinning and butchering killed animals.

an animal. Skin became clothing, bedding, or straps for sleds. Bones became tools, knives, or needles. Henson watched his new friends carefully and then tried each task on his own. It was not long before he was working alongside them with little trouble. By the end of 1891, Henson was an expert hunter, leading his own hunting parties over the snow.

The All-Important Dogsled

Driving a dogsled team was a vital skill that all of the expedition members needed to learn. It was the only way the men could carry all the supplies needed during their trek north. They could drag a sled themselves but that would quickly prove exhausting. The Inuit used teams of dogs to pull their supplies, so Peary wanted to do the same.

Even though Henson was a quick learner—and very determined—it took some time getting used to driving a team. First of all, there was the matter of controlling the dogs harnessed to the sled. It required strong arms and a strong back. The size of the team depended on the weight of the sled, but

A Dogsled Team

The Inuit used Husky dogs attached to sleds as their main source of transportation. The size of the dog team depended on the size and weight of the sled. Peary used sleds that could carry up to eight hundred pounds of supplies. These sleds required teams as large as fourteen dogs. Much smaller sleds would use smaller teams.

Traditionally, the sleds were made out of animal bones and skins. The dogs were attached to the sled by a harness, also known as a trace, which allowed the dogs room to fan out over the ice. This was useful when they were pulling a load over rough terrain, up a steep hill, or across **young ice**. The sled driver controlled the dogs and would fan them out or keep them in a straight line, depending on the conditions of the snow.

The back of the sled had two handles for the driver, who would use them to control or push the sled. Driving a dog team over rough ice was similar to working a plough. It required a great deal of strength and control. The runners on the sled were long pieces of wood or bone that rested on the bottom of the sled and resembled skis. They extended out the back so that the driver could ride on them when possible. Any extra passengers would ride in the sled itself.

The Inuit sled dogs of Greenland are very strong and have thick-layered fur. This photograph from the early 20th century shows a team of 3 dogs hitched to a sled and ready for work.

Henson usually had at least seven dogs to deal with at a time. They needed to stay in formation and at the same speed. Henson held the reins in both hands and sometimes wrapped one around his back if he needed extra support to control the dogs. If the snow and ice was smooth enough—or the dogs were running at a good speed—Henson could ride on the runners of the sled. Otherwise, he had to walk behind the sled, pushing it over the rough parts.

Henson found that not only did he learn from the Inuit, but he was also able to share his knowledge and skills as a carpenter with them to help repair or rebuild sleds. He joined them on their hunts and shared his meat and furs. Henson tried to live like an Inuit as much as possible. As Henson's friend and fellow arctic explorer Peter Freuchen said, "Unlike many of the explorers who penetrated the Arctic, Henson did not look upon the Eskimo as an inferior."

Even through the cold, dark winter, Henson kept a cheery attitude. In fact, the Inuit had a special name for him. They called him *Mahri Pahluk* (sometimes written as Miy Paluk), which meant, "Matthew, the kind one."

CHAPTER 4

The Trek Begins

When I left for home and God's Country . . .
it was with the strongest resolution to never
again! no more! forever! leave my happy home
in warmer lands.

Matthew Henson was ready. After several months of
practice, he was already an expert dogsled driver.
He was comfortable in his arctic clothing and could
communicate easily with the Inuit people. It was
extremely cold—sometimes dropping to fifty degrees
below zero—but he didn't complain. Even though
Henson knew that weather conditions would likely
worsen as they went north, he was still eager to start.

Two members of the exploration team are seen here with one of the sleds
that Henson and Peary took on their arctic journeys. The sled (also known as a
sledge) was designed to hold up to 800 pounds. Some skins and food supplies
sit on top.

Henson had carefully prepared the sleds for their journey. He started working on them while still on the *Kite* and spent much of the fall building and perfecting each one. This time, the sleds they were using were not the Inuit sleds. Peary had designed these new sleds to hold up to eight hundred pounds. The runners were lashed onto the wide body of the sled so the weight could be evenly distributed. Peary believed this would give the sled more support while banging and dragging over the rough ice.

Setting Up a Supply Line

The sleds were tested a few times throughout the year as the men traveled north along Peary's planned route in order to set up a supply line of food stores. These stores—also known as caches—held food and other supplies that the traveler could tap into along the way. With these supply stations available for the men to use, they could travel with less on their sleds. Also, if they were caught in bad weather and ran low on supplies they would know where to find more.

However, the weather proved too difficult for most of them. There were too many storms, not enough daylight, and most of the team was too inexperienced in arctic survival. By the spring of 1892—when it was finally time to leave Red Cliff House for their planned trek—there was only a partial supply line in place.

A Disappointing Start

It wasn't until May 1892 that the Peary expedition started on their journey north. John Verhoeff, the team mineralogist, stayed at Red Cliff House with Mrs. Peary. The rest of the crew loaded sleds with supplies. The content of each sled was carefully considered so there would be no extra weight carried. They

A Cache of Food

A cache was simply a hiding place where food and supplies were stored for future use. Explorers or hunters might leave a cache of food and fuel while on a trek to ensure they had enough supplies for their return journey.

To keep the food from animals, it was often stored off the ground, in trees or on top of poles, or within a pile of stones known as a cairn. Cairns were also used as landmarks so travelers could find their way. Explorers in the North often left a note explaining who built a cairn and what it signified. If an expedition reached a new record for traveling north, they would build a cairn and leave a note saying when they were there. The next explorers to find the cairn would remove the note and leave a copy for anyone else who might arrive.

This illustration shows a cairn built of piled rocks. The pole coming out of the top was to help explorers find the cairn when it was covered by snow.

At the end of a day, Henson helped build igloos for temporary shelter rather than use fabric tents. A photograph c. 1926 depicts Inuit building an igloo with blocks of ice.

didn't even pack tents to sleep in, only sleeping bags. At the end of each day's march, they would build a hut made out of blocks of snow, known as an igloo.

Unfortunately, Henson's first expedition through Greenland was a short one. The team ran into problems almost immediately. They spent their first few days trying to get over a steep ridge. In order to make a trail for the sleds, the men had to use a pickaxe to break up the hard snow and ice ahead of them. They would then return for the sled and help push it over the rough terrain as the dogs pulled. It was a very slow and difficult process by which to move their precious supplies along. Then some of the dogs became sick and died.

It was while they were readjusting the sled loads to accommodate for the lost dogs that Henson realized one of his heels was frozen. Despite all his precautions, he was suffering from **frostbite**. Henson knew that he would only slow down the rest of the crew if he stayed. So, when Peary sent Gibson back to Red Cliff House for more fuel (they had discovered that many of their tins were leaking), Henson returned with him. He had been away from camp for only a few days.

Life Among the Inuit

Although he was greatly disappointed to go back early, Henson knew he could still be of use at Red Cliff House. He could help Mrs. Peary around the camp and hunt for fresh meat. He was also glad for the opportunity to spend more time with the Inuit. "I have come to love these people," he would later write. "I know every man, woman, and child in their tribe. They are my friends and they regard me as theirs."

Henson was invited into the Inuit's homes—igloos in the winter and tents in the summer—and spent many enjoyable evenings with them away from the wind and the cold.

He was also glad for the opportunity to spend more time with the Inuit.

The Inuit were great storytellers. Henson listened to their legends and came to understand much about these people and their way of life. They entertained themselves with long, often magical, tales. Their history was not written in books. It was told to them in stories. Henson was fascinated by these evenings. Watching the Inuit react with gasps and shrieks as a storyteller turned to face them while wearing a polar bear skin was just as interesting as the story itself.

Henson often watched and sometimes participated in Inuit games. Some, like the blanket toss, were quite simple. A group formed a circle, holding a sealskin stretched tight between them. Someone rested on top of the skin and the group tossed that person into the air. Other games were much rougher, and in

Kokoyah's Jaws

In *Dark Companion*, a book he collaborated on later in life, Henson tells the story of "Kokoyah's Jaws." The Inuit of Northern Greenland believed that a devil lived below the surface of the ice in certain regions. Henson understood immediately the true source of the "Jaws" reference.

Ice sometimes cracks as a glacier moves, opening up a long deep hole known as a crevasse. There is little or no chance of surviving a fall into a crevasse, so the Inuit always watch carefully while crossing the ice. If strong winds are blowing snow, it can form a sheet of ice across the opening of a crevasse. This may look like solid ice, but it is actually quite thin. Therefore, even the most observant of teams might step where they should not—and fall right into "Kokoyah's Jaws."

Explorers must be constantly vigilant in looking for changes in the ice. A crevasse can form at any time. Unlike the crevasse pictured here, many are not visible.

The blanket toss was an Inuit activity that everyone could join in. This photograph from the early 1900s shows many participants and observers—and one man being happily tossed in the air.

Henson's opinion, quite dangerous. For one game, the Inuit linked their little fingers together and pulled as hard as they could. It finished when someone gave up, but it sometimes ended with a broken bone.

It took Henson some time to understand this aspect of Inuit life. For the most part, they were kind and generous people. They welcomed the team from the *Kite* immediately and offered help with shelter and food. They often laughed and spoke kindly to most of their visitors. As a result, Henson found it strange that these same people could then play such violent games. He learned to accept these customs, though. They were all a part of life in the North.

Then There Were Two

Henson was not the only member of the team to return early. Dr. Cook and Langdon Gibson, the ornithologist, arrived at Red Cliff House at the beginning of June. Lieutenant Peary decided it would be best if only two attempted the final leg. Because they did not know how far the land would stretch—or how long it would take them to explore the unmapped region of Northern Greenland—he wanted to conserve their supplies. Peary chose Eivind Astrup, the Norwegian student, to remain with him as they sledded into the unknown.

Everyone at Red Cliff House waited several months without any word from the explorers. The *Kite* returned at the end of July to pick them all up, but Peary and Astrup were still missing. Mrs. Peary was very worried and started to imagine the worst. Then on August 5, the two men were spotted walking toward camp. They were tired and dirty as

Mrs. Peary was very worried and started to imagine the worst.

were their dogs, and their supplies were almost gone, but they were in good spirits. Henson was excited to see them and anxious to hear about their trek.

Their mission was successful. They had discovered a high ridge—named Navy Cliff by Peary—that overlooked a large bay. On the opposite shore of Independence Bay—another name provided by Peary—there was another stretch of land. Peary hoped this "new land" would lead directly to the North Pole.

The only thing left to do was clean up their home and move the supplies back to the *Kite*. They would have to leave soon to avoid heavy ice. However, their departure was delayed when John Verhoeff disappeared. He had gone off on his own to collect rocks for his research. He expected to be away for a few days, but when he did not return, search parties were sent out after him. After five days, it was decided that they could wait no longer. A note was left for Verhoeff in Red Cliff House in case he returned. Then the *Kite* and its crew sailed for home.

It wasn't until the *Kite* had set sail that Henson realized how exhausted he actually was. It had been an exciting but very strenuous year. He decided right then and "with the strongest resolution to never again! no more! forever! leave my happy home in warmer lands." Little did he know, though, that Lieutenant Peary was already hard at work making plans for the next trip, and Henson was to be a part of it.

While on their long trek, Peary and Astrup wore the same clothes every day. This undated photograph shows Peary dressed in a similar outfit that would block the extreme cold.

Early Arctic Exploration

The earliest explorers to visit the Arctic might have been ancient Greeks. There is a record of Greek geographer Pytheas reaching Greenland's shore in 325 **B C E**. Vikings and Irish monks also landed in Greenland around 1000 **C E**. However, extensive exploration of the Arctic didn't begin until the 1800s.

Whalers following their prey into the northern waters mapped some of the islands and inlets, but it was the search for a trading route that changed how the outside world perceived the icy landscape. Expeditions led by Sir John Franklin, Henry Hudson, Martin Frobisher, and others tried to discover the **Northwest Passage** between the Atlantic and Pacific Oceans. Many islands and bays throughout the North are named after these men—the first to set eyes on them.

In the 1850s, Dr. Elisha Kane led expeditions into the Arctic in search of Sir John Franklin, a British explorer who had disappeared in 1845. Kane found no trace of the Franklin party but did chart new portions of Greenland's coast. He later published his two-volume memoir, *Arctic Explorations.*

This 1895 illustration depicts Vikings landing in Greenland c. 985. The Vikings were the first to establish a European settlement on the island.

CHAPTER 5

A Second Expedition to Greenland

*From now on it was keep on going, and keep on—
and we kept on; sometimes in the face of storms
of wind and snow that it is impossible for you
to imagine.*

By the fall off 1892, everyone from the *Kite* expedition,
except Verhoeff, was safe at home. There was little time
for rest, though. The newspapers were filled with stories
of Peary's triumphs in Greenland. His discovery of
Independence Bay and the land beyond sparked the

imagination of many people. They
wanted to hear all about these
northern adventures, and Peary
didn't want to miss this golden
opportunity. He planned to go
north again as soon as possible,
which would require raising a
great deal of money quickly.
Peary decided to go on a lecture
tour and wanted Henson to
come along.

In an undated photograph, Henson
is dressed in his arctic furs, just as he
was while on tour with Peary.

Unfortunately, the year of living in ice and snow had lasting effects on Henson. He was suffering from snow blindness. This was a real danger while in the North. The sun reflecting off the white snow was very bright—especially during the long weeks of nearly constant daylight—and could easily damage one's eyes. Unfortunately, the team did not have the special glasses that the Inuit wore to protect their eyesight. These were made out of whalebone and had very thin slits to look through.

Dr. Frederick Cook, their physician in the North, offered Henson a place to stay while recuperating and arranged for him to visit an eye specialist. Henson appreciated the doctor's generosity.

Henson was extremely tired from his time in the Arctic. He desperately wanted a rest—and his wife Eva wanted him home— but Peary needed him. Henson sensed that if he didn't help Peary now he might not have the chance to go north again. As soon as he felt well enough, he joined Peary on his lecture tour.

On Tour with Peary

To generate publicity and excitement, Henson dressed in his arctic furs and drove a dog-sled team into a town. He called out, "Huk! Huk!" just as the Inuit had taught him and snapped the reins. The dogs responded to his command. Crowds gathered along the street, waving and cheering as he passed. Henson drove the team into the lecture hall and

A 1995 photograph shows an Inuit man wearing a pair of snow glasses to help protect his eyes against long exposures to sunlight.

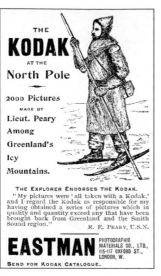

Peary was a well-known figure in 19th-century America. So much so that Kodak Cameras hired him as a spokesman for this 1893 newspaper advertisement—even though he had not yet reached the North Pole as depicted in the ad.

onto the stage. He then took his place *behind* Peary.

Peary gave his talk, enthralling the audience with tales of bitter storms, kind Inuits, and exploring new land. Henson sat quietly behind him with his dogs. The audience could look to him as a living example of Peary's arctic adventure, but he was not asked to speak.

It was a hectic tour—with Peary giving 165 lectures in 103 days—and a great success. He made as much as $2,000 for a single performance. Peary's fame was steadily growing. Henson, on the other hand, was only rarely mentioned. Once again, he was only referred to as Peary's manservant, if at all. All of the work he had done building their shelter and the sleds, hunting, fishing, and being a skilled interpreter were not acknowledged. Henson thought that his chance for fame and recognition would come one day. He only had to wait.

Return to Greenland

In the spring of 1893, Peary announced that enough money had been raised. He hired another ship—the *Falcon*—to take them north again. They left from Philadelphia in June with a much larger team, including Mrs. Peary, who was expecting their first child in September. On August 3, the *Falcon* arrived in Bowdoin Bay, just south of McCormick Bay.

The *Falcon*, pictured here in a photograph dated 1915, took Peary's much larger crew north in 1893.

Peary's plans were much more ambitious for this expedition. He would take his eight-man crew across Greenland's **ice cap** to Independence Bay. From there, three men would go north to investigate the land on the far side of the bay. Peary hoped it would be a direct path to the North Pole. Three other men would go southeast and explore that coastline. Two other men would make a camp at Navy Cliff near the bay. They would hunt and store meat for the northern parties' return to ensure it had enough supplies to reach Bowdoin Bay again.

However, there was a lot of work to do before then. Once again, their first task was to build a new shelter for the winter. Anniversary Lodge was made much larger than Red Cliff House in order to accommodate more men. It was finished in mid-August and just in the nick of time. Ice was already forming in the bay. The heavy snows wouldn't be far behind.

Henson and the others soon realized that they had made a serious mistake with their shelter. Anniversary Lodge was built with a glass roof, and heat from the stove was escaping through it. Also, the roof was not strong enough to hold all the snow and was in danger of collapsing. Henson covered the glass roof with wood to strengthen it. As it was a harsh winter with a heavy snowfall, the team had to shovel it regularly to keep weight off the roof.

Then, on October 31, a large iceberg broke off from one of the glaciers and created a tremendous wave that crashed against the shore. When the wall of water retreated, it carried most of the barrels of fuel oil with it and washed them into the bay. The men were only able to retrieve a small portion. With their fuel supply so low, they were forced to burn **walrus blubber** instead. The burned blubber provided heat but not always enough. When the inside walls weren't covered in black soot from the burning fat, they were covered in a sheet of ice, sometimes several inches thick.

As this photograph shows, the view over the polar ice cap is white with snow and ice as far as the eye can see.

Even though Henson tried not to worry, he knew that the team was much larger than the previous crew, and more people meant more supplies. They had already lost much of their fuel oil, and the difficult weather hindered them further. Storms through the fall not only hampered their hunting trips but also kept them from spending much time outside for their preparations. The weather also made if difficult to train with the dogsled teams. Of all the team members, only Henson and Astrup, the Norwegian student from the previous trek, had been in the far North before. Henson began to wonder if they were ill-prepared.

A teenaged Marie Peary (right) and her mother are photographed in Sydney, Nova Scotia, in 1909.

The news was not all terrible though. Mrs. Peary gave birth to a little girl—Marie Ahnighito—on September 12, 1893. The Inuit called her the "Snow Baby," and she was quite the attraction. Inuit traveled from far and wide to see little Marie, bringing her presents and warm clothes.

Another Hard Lesson Learned

The teams of eight men, twelve sleds, and ninety dogs left Anniversary Lodge on March 6, 1894. Five Inuit joined them, although they only planned to go as far as the ice cap. Rather than build igloos at the end of each day's march, Peary intended to use tents, which would add considerable weight to the already overloaded sleds. There was only a meager supply line in place as the difficult autumn had prevented team members from finding and filling the caches. Then, less than a week into the trek, they ran into further problems.

Two dogs came down with *piblokto*, a madness caused by the snow and cold, and had to be put down. Then Astrup became ill with food poisoning, and Hugh Lee, a young newspaperman in the North for the first time, announced his foot was frozen. Both returned to Anniversary Lodge, leaving Peary with a six-man crew.

Piblokto

Piblokto is an Inuit word for a temporary insanity caused by life on the ice and snow. Some of the symptoms of piblokto in a

human include howling or screaming, removing clothes in the extreme cold outside, and sometimes a deep depression. Usually this condition does not last. Someone suffering from piblokto usually recovers fully after a short time.

It's a different story when a dog is struck by piblokto. While Henson and Peary made their treks, the dogs often suffered after a fall through the ice. They would then howl, attack other dogs, and thrash about on the snow. Dogs suffering from piblokto are usually not expected to recover and are put down.

A 19th-century wood engraving shows an Inuit camp with their dogs. The animals worked hard for their masters and in return were well cared for. It was a sorrowful time when a dog came down with piblokto and had to be put down.

On March 22, a blizzard struck. Henson and his teammates were trapped in the tents for thirty-six hours in temperatures that dropped to sixty degrees below zero. When they finally emerged after the storm, Henson noticed that some of the men had gotten frostbite. Anyone who could not continue was sent back to Anniversary Lodge.

There were only five men left. Peary's plan of separating the team at Navy Cliff was now impossible. They still faced terrible storms and high winds and their food supply was dangerously low. Peary had to admit defeat. On April 10—while 128 miles from Anniversary Lodge—the lieutenant announced they were turning back. They left a cache of food and a bamboo marker and started the long trek back.

A Change of Plans

More than a week later, they arrived at Anniversary Lodge. Henson was exhausted. His eyes were hurting from the sun's glare on the snow, and he could feel the effects of frostbite on his face and feet. He was also dirty and covered in lice.

Despite all his careful planning, Peary had failed in his mission to explore the north and eastern coast of Greenland. Henson knew the lieutenant would be worried about raising funds for future expeditions. Henson was only mildly surprised when a few days later Peary announced he was remaining in Greenland and would return to Navy Cliff and explore north the following year. Henson was very quick to say he would stay, too.

When the *Falcon* returned in August 1894, Peary, Henson, and Hugh Lee remained while the rest went home, including Mrs. Peary and daughter Marie. Henson sent word back to his wife, hoping that she would understand.

The team was still low on supplies. The extended stay was unplanned, so the *Falcon* did not bring extra food or fuel. The three men would have to find other resources. Henson wasn't worried, though. He had learned a great deal about arctic living over the past few years, and he had faith in the lieutenant as team leader. Henson felt certain that their trek in the new year would bring them success.

Peary left a cairn, similar to the one shown here at Cape Sheridan, before returning to Anniversary Lodge. This cairn, photographed in 1945, was discovered by U.S. Army officers and contained records of Peary's expedition. The R stands for the *Roosevelt*, Peary's ship that was built in 1905.

CHAPTER 6

Difficult Years in the North

. . . The recollections of the long race with death across the 450 miles of the ice-cap of North Greenland in 1895, with Commander Peary and Hugh Lee, are still the most vivid.

Having made the decision to stay in Greenland for another year, Henson set out to replenish their supplies. By this time, he was an accomplished hunter and enjoyed his time with the Inuit searching for food. As Peary said, "Henson, with his years of arctic experience, was almost as skillful at this work as an Eskimo."

The three-man crew and a group of Inuit attempted to find the cache left in the spring, but were unsuccessful. The bamboo pole that Peary left as a marker had disappeared. Also, storms continued to rage through the interior, and they were again forced back to Anniversary Lodge.

Starting on the Trek North

On April 1, 1895, the three men set off once again. They left with six Inuit, three sleds, and sixty dogs. The sleds were loaded with their remaining supplies—biscuits, tea, condensed milk, some fresh meat, tins of pea soup, and pemmican, a nutritious meat mixture. They had small stoves to heat up their tea, but Peary wanted them to avoid cooking too many meals. He worried that cooking would use up much of the fuel. Also, he still had hopes of

Dining at the North Pole

Extreme cold can preserve goods for many years. This 1993 photograph shows supplies in the hut of Ernest Shackleton, a South Pole explorer of Antarctica. These items were left there 80 years earlier.

Any food brought on an expedition had to be easily transportable and highly nutritious. It was also important that it would not go bad too quickly. Canned goods worked well. Explorers brought canned beans, pea soup, and condensed milk because they provided protein and energy and were easy to prepare. All meals were cooked on a simple stove using alcohol for fuel.

Dried fruit, such as raisins, were brought along as sweet treats.

Pemmican was perfect for long journeys. It was made out of pounded meat, dried berries, and fat. It lasted a long time before going bad and was nutritious. This was not an Inuit delicacy. It was first made by northern Inuit Americans and was a staple in the explorer's or fur trader's diet. Before leaving on the trek across the ice cap in 1895, Henson, Peary, and Lee made their own pemmican.

Despite the fact that Henson and Peary were surrounded by snow—and snow is essentially frozen water—they couldn't use snow to quench their thirst. They had to boil the water first. Therefore, tea was the best way to prevent **dehydration**. Once again, it was easy to transport and easy to prepare.

finding the missing cache of food along the way.

Henson's sled contained the carefully loaded navigational equipment. Quite literally, they would be lost without it. They carried a compass and pocket **sextant**. By taking readings along the way, measuring the longitude (the north/south lines on a map) and latitude (the east/west lines on a map), they could determine how far they had come. Perhaps most importantly, they would know their distance from the North Pole.

One needs a steady hand and keen eye to use a sextant. This 1911 newspaper illustration shows the Norwegian explorer Roald Amundsen lying on the snow to measure the horizon.

Henson had become acquainted with the mechanics of navigation while at sea. He had watched Captain Childs take readings with his sextant and record the information in his log. Peary used the same method to determine their position on the ice cap and beyond.

Henson also learned to navigate by using "dead reckoning," a technique that did not require special tools or equipment, only practice and experience. By knowing how far they traveled and by matching the sun or moon to the horizon, he could determine their position without using a sextant.

Navigating by "dead reckoning" required extensive experience. This photograph—taken during his 1908–1909 expedition—shows Peary using a telescope to scan the horizon.

Trouble Along the Way

As Peary, Henson, and Lee headed northeast from camp, they met with problems early on. Once again, they couldn't find the food cache, and the Inuit turned back before reaching the ice cap. Bad weather still plagued them. Wind and snow whipped around them, making it easy to lose their way. It was during one of these storms that Lee fell so far behind that he became lost.

The weather was too dangerous to look for him right away, so Henson built an igloo. He and Peary waited several days, listening for Lee's voice amid the howling wind.

When there was a break in the weather, Henson searched for Lee. He had almost given up hope when he saw a sled approaching from a distance. Lee was in very bad shape. He was delirious and in desperate need of food and rest. Lee's feet were so badly frostbitten that he couldn't walk. He would have to ride on a sled for the rest of the journey.

Henson attached one sled behind another, forming a train. He then assembled the dogs from both sleds into one large team. They continued on their way, pushing through the wind and over the ice.

Many of the sled dogs were suffering under the strain of their cold trek. At the end of each day's march, Henson walked among the pack. He picked out the weakest ones and put them out of their misery. He then fed the meat to the other dogs. Henson hated this part of his job but knew it was necessary. Without this unfortunate task, all of the dogs would perish from exhaustion and hunger.

By the time they reached Navy Cliff—the glacier along Independence Bay that Peary discovered in 1892—they were dangerously low on food. They were now 600 miles from Anniversary Lodge and had only eleven dogs left. Even though he was terribly exhausted, it was time for Henson to go hunting. After making Lee as comfortable as possible in a tent, Henson and Peary traveled back down the glacier on a sled. They went into a canyon where they hoped to find some game.

Hunting for Food

The dogs were the first to notice them. They could smell the musk oxen in the canyon before either man saw the herd. Henson tied up all the dogs but kept the leader with him for the hunt.

As Henson moved in closer to the herd with the lead dog next to him, Peary readied his rifle. Henson released the lead dog, and the animal ran into the canyon, barking and growling. It ran a wide circle around the herd and continued on this path making tighter and tighter circles and closing the herd in on itself. With each circle, the Husky moved in closer, nipping at the heels of the musk oxen, and snarling. The herd packed together until they stood in one tight group.

While the dog was bringing the herd in, Henson and Peary moved in closer as well. As Henson tells the story in *Dark Companion*, Peary fired the first shot, hitting one of the bulls.

Other explorers also hunted musk ox while crossing Greenland. This photograph was taken during Dr. Cook's 1908 polar expedition as he hunted for food with Inuit companions.

Both men continued to fire shots into the herd. Suddenly, one of the musk oxen charged at Peary. The lieutenant was having trouble loading his rifle with the animal barreling toward him. He was still struggling when another shot rang out and the musk ox dropped in its tracks. Henson had saved Peary's life with his quick response.

Using the skills the Inuit had taught him, Henson began to skin and butcher the meat. It was difficult to concentrate since he was so hungry but after a few days—and several meals—they were ready to return to Lee. Henson used a musk-ox hide as a sled to pull the remaining meat behind them.

When they returned to Navy Cliff, they discovered that Lee was so weak he could barely eat the meal Henson

An Alaskan Inuit poses for a photograph in the early 20th century while holding snowshoes. These shoes, which enabled a person to walk on snow-covered grounds, have the same design as those worn by Henson and company.

prepared. His meager food rations had run out a day or two earlier. He was in remarkably good spirits, though, and his frostbitten feet had improved with a week of rest. Lee insisted that he was feeling much better and able to walk on his own using his snowshoes. He did just that as they went back down the glacier.

Starting Back

With supplies low and Lee in bad shape, Peary decided it would be irresponsible to continue on this trek, so he decided to give up on his quest to explore the land north of Independence Bay. If they were lucky, and their 600-mile journey home was problem-free, their musk-oxen meat might be enough to sustain them the entire way.

Alas, the poor weather and their bad luck continued. Swirling snow in the bright and constant sunlight often blinded them. Finally, when they were still 200 miles from Anniversary Lodge, the musk-oxen meat ran out. Henson knew they had no other choice. After they set up their shelter for the night he walked among the dog team. With great sorrow, and a very heavy heart, he killed eight of the nine dogs. Without this meat, the men would never make it back.

It was still a struggle over the ice, and Lee's strength finally gave out 120 miles from the lodge. Henson helped him onto the sled. However, the remaining dog was too weak to pull the heavy sled, so Henson and Peary threw the dog leashes over their shoulders and began pulling the sled themselves. They all moved very slowly through the wind and snow.

The three men had been without food for two days when they finally reached Anniversary Lodge on June 25, 1895. Henson was numb from the cold and astonished that they made it back alive. His feet were swollen and in great pain. They all suffered from frostbite and windburn.

Although they were at last in their arctic home, Henson did not feel secure. They had only a few cans of beans left, no dog team to assist in a hunt, and they were all too weak to travel any distance. It was late June and the *Falcon* wasn't due to return until August. Henson wondered if his luck had finally run out.

Rescued

Henson was in such a weakened state that he could barely move or focus his weary eyes, but he noticed someone—or something—moving about the lodge. It took him some time to realize it was some of his Inuit friends. They were caring for the other two, nursing them back to health.

They tended to Henson as well and gave him something warm to drink. It was dark red and tasted awful but he drank it all. It wasn't until he recovered that they told him the drink was— blood of a seal! Henson was horrified but admitted that it likely saved his life.

During their weeks of recovery, Peary started to rethink his route to the pole. He determined that the problem was trying to cross so much land and ice in such a short time. If they could land much farther north on the coast of Greenland—farther than either McCormick or Bowdoin Bay—closer to the Polar Sea, then they would have less distance to travel on foot and sled. He was confident that this was the answer to the North Pole mystery.

This map of Greenland and its surrounding areas shows the destination points of the first two expeditions by Peary and Henson. On both occasions—in 1892 and 1895—they traveled as far as Independence Bay and Navy Cliff.

CHAPTER 7

The Find at Cape York

As usual I was a member of the party, and my back still aches when I think of the hard work I did to help load that monster aboard the Hope.

While Peary was excited by his new plan, he was frustrated by his predicament: The *Falcon* would soon arrive to pick them up, and they would be heading home defeated. While their lack of discoveries tormented Peary, Henson came up with a perfect solution: They could take back the **meteorites** located at Cape York, a site on the west coast of Greenland, south of Anniversary Lodge. The "space rocks" would impress any investor. Peary agreed that it was a marvelous idea.

Henson was speaking about three large meteorites near Cape York that were first mentioned by John Ross, a British explorer, in 1818. These meteorites had landed in Greenland about ten thousand years ago and were thought to be four-and-a-half-billion years old. No visitor—European or American— had seen them since Ross's discovery. The Inuit considered the meteorites sacred so they were secretive about their exact location.

John Ross was the first European to mention the meteorites at Cape York. In 1818 he led the navy's first major expedition to sail the Northwest Passage.

Finding the Meteorites

Peary and Henson knew exactly where to look, though. They had already seen them. In the spring of 1894—when the men had decided to stay another year—they set out to find the legendary rocks.

According to some accounts, including *A Negro Explorer At The North Pole,* it was Peary and Lee who had journeyed south. According to *Dark Companion,* however, Henson had accompanied Peary.

With Henson acting as interpreter, Peary bribed an Inuit man to take them to the meteorites. Of course, finding the meteorites was not as easy as that. Their first guide grew anxious about taking the visitors to the sacred spot, so he abandoned them along the way. Henson had to find another willing Inuit and convince him to help.

The ground at Cape York was still covered in snow, and they had to dig down to find the rocks. The meteorites were clearly large, but it was hard to say how big because much of them were embedded so deeply in the ground.

Now it was the summer of 1895, and they needed to find a way to bring the meteorites home before winter set in.

It was the *Kite* that arrived in August, not the *Falcon,* to pick them up. Lee, who was still not well, was brought onto the ship and set up in a cabin. Henson loaded their supplies onto the *Kite* and said good-bye to his friends before the team sailed south along the coast. They stopped at Cape York.

Each of the meteorites had been given a name: "The Woman" weighed two-and-a-half tons, "The Dog" was half a ton, and "The Tent" weighed approximately thirty-five tons—one of the largest known meteorites in the world.

Retrieving the Meteorites

Using a hawser, a thick cable used for towing boats, and a makeshift sled of timber, the *Kite's* crew, along with Peary, Henson, and some Inuit workers pulled the two smaller meteorites—The Dog and The Woman—on board. The Tent would have to wait. They couldn't pry it out of the earth, which was probably just as well. The *Kite* was not as large a ship as the *Falcon*, and they didn't want to overload it.

When the team arrived home in September 1895, the meteorites caused a huge sensation. The **American Museum of Natural History** in New York bought them from Peary for $40,000.

The museum was also excited to hear that there was another—even larger one—still to come.

Peary chartered a ship—the *Hope*—in the summer of 1896 to return to Cape York. Henson, of course, went with him.

The *Hope* was trapped by ice in Baffin Bay, so the team carried their supplies across the ice from ship to shore. After a tremendous amount of work digging the largest meteorite from

After digging into the rocky ground, it took a team of men to pull "The Dog" to the surface. This 1895 photograph shows the ship's crew and Inuit working together.

the earth, Peary had to leave it on shore. He and his team could not carry The Tent to the ship, and floating it on an ice floe was too dangerous. If the ice broke or tipped, the meteorite would be lost forever. The ice was strong enough

However, Peary did not trust the ice under the weight of the meteorite.

to carry the men and their equipment. If there were cracks in the sheets of ice, they could easily jump from one floe to the other. However, Peary did not trust the ice under the weight of the meteorite. There were too many cracks and it felt too thin. He decided to try again the following year.

So, once again, Peary, Henson, and the *Hope* returned to Cape York in the summer of 1897. This time the men were successful. They loaded the meteorite into the hold of the *Hope* and took it back to America. The American Museum of Natural

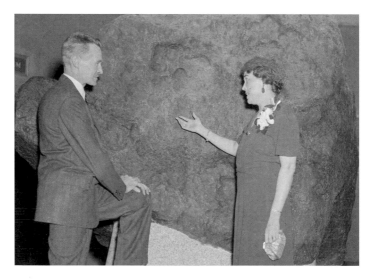

Forty years after arriving in America, the meteorites still made news. Peary's children—Marie and Robert—pose in front of The Tent—before giving a talk at the Polar Society in 1939.

More Than Artifacts for the Museum

This photograph—taken c. 1898—shows Minik Wallace in western style dress.

Peary brought back much more than furs, dogs, and meteorites from Greenland. He returned with animals, bones, and Inuit artifacts. Most of these he sold to museums to raise money.

In 1897, he brought back a group of six Inuit, leaving them with the Museum of Natural History. The museum wanted the opportunity to study the Inuit people closely. Unfortunately, within a year, four of the Inuit had died from tuberculosis and one had returned to Greenland. Minik, the remaining Inuit, was only seven years old.

He was eventually adopted by William Wallace, the curator at the museum, and lived in Wallace's home until the young Inuit was sixteen years old. Minik then wanted to go back to Greenland. He and some members of the press insisted that Peary take responsibility. Peary claimed he had done nothing wrong in bringing the boy to America, but eventually he agreed to help Minik with his journey home.

History bought The Tent, completing their collection of the Cape York meteorites.

Until the Inuit started trading with Europeans, these meteorites were their only source of metal. They would chip off pieces and use them to create knives and other tools. Unfortunately, the Inuit had no say in the removal of the meteorites, and after all the rocks were moved, they were now solely reliant on trade to obtain metal of any kind.

Support was high for Peary again, and he quickly used the meteorites to his advantage with fund-raising. He wanted to get moving as soon as possible. Earlier on, the crew of the *Kite* had brought upsetting news for Peary. Norwegian explorer Fridtjof Nansen had recently attempted to reach the pole but turned back 230 miles from the prize. Peary worried that his chances for glory and for reaching the North Pole were slipping away.

Peary now decided that he was going farther north the following summer. This time, he was not coming back until he had reached the North Pole!

Fridtjof Nansen came close to reaching the North Pole before Peary. He was known for more than exploration though. He won the Nobel Peace Prize in 1922, largely for his work with refugees after World War I.

CHAPTER 8

Making a Home in the North

Many and many a time, for periods covering more than twelve months, I have been to all intents an Esquimo.

Between the time when the *Kite* returned to New York in September of 1895 and the time when Henson and Peary returned to Cape York to retrieve the final meteorite (The Tent), Henson thought he was about to face unemployment once again. He no longer had work with the navy, and there were no lecture tours for him to accompany Peary on. Luckily, work found him.

The American Museum of Natural History where Henson worked is shown in this c. 1913 photograph.

Working for the Museum

The Museum of Natural History in New York City had a good relationship with Peary. Its president, Morris K. Jessup, was one of the lieutenant's strongest supporters. The museum also paid for many of the specimens that Peary's expeditions brought back from the North, including the meteorites.

Thanks to the skills he had learned with the Inuit to skin and preserve animal pelts, Henson was hired to help with the museum's arctic displays. They were mounting the bodies of animals Peary's team had brought back and wanted to depict lifelike scenes of Greenland. Henson could offer a unique perspective.

This was a positive time for Henson. Suddenly, his voice and opinion truly mattered. Henson worked with the museum, helping with their displays for three years. He took leaves of absence during the summers of 1896 and 1897 when Peary needed him in Cape York.

Over the years, Henson had proved time and time again that he would go anywhere that Peary needed him. However, he did not have the same relationship with his wife Eva. They had been married for six years and Henson had spent most of that time in Greenland. When he returned from Cape York with the last meteorite, Henson and Eva decided to divorce.

Making Their Way to the North, Again

It was also in the fall of 1897 that Otto Sverdrup, another Norwegian explorer, announced that he planned to make a run for the pole. To make matters worse, Peary claimed that Sverdrup planned to use the lieutenant's route. He would land far north and cross the Polar Sea with the assistance of the Inuit and dog teams.

Peary considered Otto Sverdrup a rival for the North Pole. This photo of Sverdrup was taken aboard the *Fram* during Nansen's 1893–1896 journey to reach the pole.

Peary was furious. It was an unwritten rule that one explorer would not trespass on another's plan. With support from the public and scientific communities, Peary acted quickly. His next expedition would be the most elaborate plan yet. This time he would stay in the North for at least four years—and this time he would reach the North Pole at last!

Without giving a second's thought, Henson agreed to go. He had no doubt that Peary would one day make it to the pole, and it was Henson's goal to be right beside him.

Two ships went north with Peary's expedition in July 1898. The *Hope* carried Peary, Henson, and their team from America while the *Windward* sailed from England with more supplies. Both ships met in Etah, a settlement north of McCormick Bay, in mid-August. All supplies from the *Hope* were then transported to the *Windward* and the *Hope* returned to America. Henson went ashore at Etah to recruit Inuit to go farther north with them.

This time, Peary's team was much smaller and the running of the expedition would be more complex but streamlined. There was only Peary, Henson, the expedition's physician, Dr. Thomas Dedrick, the captain of the *Windward,* John Bartlett, and his assistant and nephew, Robert Bartlett. The men didn't even bring timber on the ship to build a winter shelter. The team would live on the *Windward* instead. If they were going to survive over such a long time, they would need to model much of their living practices after the Inuit. They didn't want to take any chances, which meant dressing like them as well.

Peary wasn't the first to adapt Inuit ways, but he was clever enough to give this practice a name. "The Peary System," as he called it, required that the team dress, live, and travel like the Inuit. They wore arctic furs, built igloos for shelter rather than use tents, slept in their fur clothing rather than sleeping bags, and learned to hunt and eat like the Inuit. Peary had long insisted that each member of his team learn to drive a dog-sled team, and Henson understood the wisdom behind it. It was the fastest way to cross the snow, and if dogs died during the trek, they could be used to feed the other dogs. As Henson learned in 1895, if supplies ran out, the men could eat the dogs, too. It might be their only means of survival in an inhospitable climate.

> *"The Peary System," as he called it, required that they dress, live, and travel like the Inuit.*

The new crew—especially Robert Bartlett—would play an important role in future expeditions. This 1909 photograph shows Peary (left) and Robert Bartlett in Battle Harbor, Labrador.

Improper Clothing for Arctic Exploration

Even before Peary's time, the British sent many expeditions into the North to search for the Northwest Passage. Unfortunately, they were often sent into the Arctic with wool coats and mittens. They thought it would be degrading to dress or live in any style but their own. Such sentiments were a reflection of the racism and arrogance that often fueled early exploration. It was almost impossible to dry out wet wool in freezing temperatures. It provided no insulation, and the wind whipped right through it. To solve the insulation problem, the British government gave their men metal hot-water bottles to stuff under their coats. The water and container quickly froze leaving the men with a block of ice against their skin. They also wore leather boots that froze, cracked, and broke open, exposing their feet to the elements.

An imagined account of Sir John Franklin's last days on the ice. The engraving shows the crew succumbing to the cold in their wool caps and coats.

The *Windward*—reloaded with supplies collected from the *Hope* and Etah, Inuit families, and dogs—sailed toward Cape Sheridan on the northern tip of Ellesmere Island, which lay west of Greenland. The ice in Kane Basin was too thick, though, and they were forced to land in Cape D'Urville. This meant they were faced with the same problem as in previous years. The men were too far south, and there was simply too much land to cross. If they didn't have a good hunting season that fall, they would likely run out of food before reaching the pole.

Thankfully, Peary had a back-up plan. The exploration team would carry their supplies by sled to Fort Conger, on the northeastern coast of Ellesmere Island. They would later cross the strait between Ellesmere and Greenland when it was frozen over. The team could easily, or so they hoped, make their way to the pole from there. Perhaps most importantly, there was a deserted U.S. Army base at Fort Conger, which meant there would likely be supplies.

Setting Up a Supply Line

In order to reach Fort Conger, a 250-mile supply line would have to be set up. This was a much longer distance than anything Peary's teams had attempted in the past. He knew it was going to be a very difficult job and trusted only one man to lead the way. In November 1898, Henson, four Inuit men, and two dog-sled teams started north.

The ice was very rough, and it was difficult to break a trail. Polar ice is not smooth and flat. It does not look like a skating rink or roadway. The ice is formed by snow swirling in the wind and then freezing. This creates a bumpy, jagged landscape with many dips and valleys. The lead sled would have to break a path through these icy peaks.

There were constant problems with the sleds. Every day, something else broke. Every day, Henson made repairs, trying to make them last the long trek. When they had traveled just over a hundred miles, Henson realized they could get no farther. They turned back to the *Windward*.

Henson was surprised upon their return to see Sverdrup leaving the ship. Henson found Peary in his cabin. The lieutenant was furious. The Norwegian explorer had just informed Peary that he was planning to winter at Fort Conger, as well.

He told Henson that they must push their way north as quickly as possible. Peary wasn't going to let anyone beat him.

Finding Their Way to Fort Conger

It was just after Christmas—during the mostly dark days of winter—that Peary, Henson, and four Inuit men set out again for Fort Conger. It seemed like they would never have the luck of good weather. It was yet another trek slowed down by bad storms and rough terrain. Even though he found many joys in his work, Henson had to admit that exploration was a difficult career choice.

It was too dark to use a sextant, so they relied on the Inuit's experience over the ice and Henson's dead-reckoning skills. He watched for the ridges that lined the coast and followed them as the team moved north along Ellesmere. The men knew they were over water when they could feel the ice moving. Still miles from the destination, their food supply ran out. The men struggled through the dark, barely able to see a few feet in front of them, and were disoriented from the temperatures of sixty below zero.

Finally, the team found a cairn. The note inside said that Conger was just a couple of miles to the west. The marker had done its job: It directed travelers to safety.

On January 6, 1899, they arrived at Fort Conger. It was

still dark so the men had to grope their way around the building. They were relieved to have found shelter and pleased to discover that Sverdrup wasn't waiting for them.

No one had set foot in the building since the former U.S. Army company of men had left fifteen years before. The building at Fort Conger was divided into two rooms and both were a complete mess. Whatever was left behind was strewn everywhere. Dishes and discarded clothing were scattered about the rooms. Tea, coffee, and other food stores were spilled on floors and tables. It looked like the servicemen had left in a hurry, only grabbing essentials and leaving the rest.

Although this drawing of Fort Conger was made 17 years earlier, little had changed when Peary and Henson arrived. Isolation and cold had preserved the building almost perfectly.

Henson searched through the supplies and found some food. He laughed to himself. There was one advantage to the arctic freeze: The food was still good. For that brief moment, Henson felt a great relief.

A Severe Case of Frostbite

As Henson tells the story in *Dark Companion*, he noticed that Peary was limping and in pain. He lit a fire then helped

Peary remove his *kamiks*, or boots. Both men feared the worst, and they were right. Peary's toes on both feet were badly frostbitten from the long journey to Fort Conger. Peary needed immediate care to prevent gangrene—a life-threatening infection of the flesh.

As Peary drank a cupful of rum, Henson tended to the lieutenant's feet. The drink warmed Peary up and helped dull the pain. In an attempt to save the damaged toes, Henson soaked Peary's feet in a bowl of water and iodine crystals, which helped to clean the wound and prevent infection.

As Peary drank a cupful of rum, Henson tended to the lieutenant's feet.

The lieutenant spent several weeks on a cot while recovering. Henson knew that he needed to get Peary back to the *Windward* for medical attention as soon as possible.

It should be noted here that both Peary and Dr. Dedrick claimed in their individual diaries that the doctor was with them on this trek, and it was the doctor who primarily cared for Peary, not Henson. In later interviews, Henson also claimed that he amputated Peary's toes at Fort Conger, but most sources— including the diaries—state that Dendrick removed Peary's damaged toes when they returned to the ship.

Differences aside, though, Henson's point when retelling the story still stands. The elements were harsh, injury was always a possibility, and the need to persevere was necessary. Peary and Henson had set their sights on a very difficult goal. Every stop along the way to the North Pole brought potential danger. They would have to bravely face them all.

While waiting in the long darkness for Peary's feet to heal, Henson continued to scavenge for food. He would never forget those days. Even with the provisions left at Conger, they needed fresh meat, especially Peary. Henson hunted, cooked, cared for the dogs, and tended to Peary.

Because Peary had difficulty walking across the snow—even in snowshoes—he would have to ride on a sled. Henson either pulled the sled with the dogs over the very rough ice or drove the dog team while Peary rode on the sled.

According to Henson, this marked a change in his relationship with Peary. Up to this point, Peary had relied on Henson's assistance for most things around the camp: cooking when necessary, carpentry, repairs, and hunting. He had also needed Henson as an interpreter. Now, however, he needed Henson for the physical day-to-day activities. Until Peary was capable of moving about with little or no assistance, he had to rely almost completely on Henson.

Returning to Etah

The *Windward* did not break free of the ice until August of 1899—after almost a year had passed. The ship returned Peary and Henson (and Dedrick, according to accounts other than Henson's) to the settlement of Etah, Greenland, and then sailed home without them. It was not scheduled to return until 1901. They were facing another two years alone in the North, living among the Inuit.

Henson wasn't too troubled. He felt at home in the North and with the Inuit. He considered them family. He worried that it was different for Peary though. The lieutenant did not speak the Inuit's language. He did not have the same companionship with them; and now, his injured feet limited Peary. His feet had healed fully from the surgery, but walking without toes was still difficult, and this caused him a great deal of discomfort. He could only walk or work for so long before the pain was unbearable.

More Attempts

In the fall of 1899, Henson and Peary returned to Fort Conger with several Inuit families. For their remaining time in the North, the men would use Conger as their advanced base to the pole.

Most of their provisions had been brought north the previous spring via a supply line.

It was from Fort Conger that the two men set out for the pole in April 1900. They left with five Inuit men and seven sleds. Peary's route took them across the frozen strait to Greenland. They were headed to the strip of land he first spotted by Independence Bay in 1892. They would explore that stretch as long as they could—hopefully, all the way to the pole.

They faced their usual dilemmas of harsh winds, bitter cold, and rough ice. Dogs fell into water, and there was little game to be found as their food supply dwindled. On April 14, 1900, they reached the northernmost point of Greenland—proving at last that it was an island. However, they were still 400 miles from the pole with only the frozen Polar Sea between them and their ultimate goal.

They mapped the northern coast of Greenland, which was an important contribution, but not the prize that Peary sought. Again, without enough food, they turned back to Fort Conger—disappointed but not defeated.

They mapped the coast of Greenland, which was an important contribution, but not the prize that Peary sought.

Yet, they continued. They spent their summers in Etah and each winter at Fort Conger. At the beginning of the New Year, they made another run for the pole. They were able get a bit farther each year but always turned back due to hunger and bad weather. They were pleased with their progress; however, the series of attempts was nearly killing them. In March 1902, they set another record for reaching the farthest north before turning back.

Peary finally had to admit that it was time to go home. It was upsetting to return to America before reaching the pole, but the men were exhausted. They would need rest and a new plan to make the next attempt successful. Even though he felt disheartened, Peary was not ready to give up. He would continue on his quest, and Henson would be at his side.

Following their 1892 and 1895 expeditions to Independence Bay, Peary and Henson made three more treks: retrieving the meteorites at Cape York in 1895, then arriving at Greenland's most northern tip in 1900, and finally reaching a record of farthest north in 1902.

CHAPTER 9

Back in America

The Roosevelt *was built with a knowledge of the
requirements of Arctic navigation, gained by the
experience of an American on six former voyages
into the Arctic.*
—Robert E. Peary

Henson and Peary parted ways when the *Windward* docked
in New York City in the fall of 1902. Henson was back in
America for the first time in four years. He was home. At
least that's what he kept reminding himself. The truth was he
had moved so many times that nowhere felt like home.

He was missing his life in the Arctic, the other team
members, and his close Inuit friends whom he considered
his adopted family. He hadn't lived in America for a
significant amount of time in more than a decade. He didn't
feel any ties to one place or a single person. Henson was
feeling very much a stranger in his own country.

The lieutenant was anxious to start fund-raising for the
next campaign but couldn't tell Henson how long it might
take. He promised to get in touch as soon as he had a new
date to sail.

Peary hoped they would be gone again by the following
summer.

Of course, there were no guarantees. Henson knew that it
might take longer to drum up support this time. He was thirty-
six years old, and needed to find his own source of income.
He could not afford to wait for word that might not come.

Traveling Through America

Henson realized that he wasn't ready to settle into city life after living in the Arctic. He decided he needed a change of careers.

He had sailed the globe and lived in the Arctic but he had barely seen any of his own country. Henson realized there was a way to earn a living and see America. He found work as a Pullman porter on the railroad.

Henson fell in love with America's beauty. He worked on several different railway lines and was able to travel through the Northeast, the Midwest, and finally the South. It was a great opportunity to see the varied landscape and experience the country firsthand. Unfortunately, this new job also brought less desirable elements into Henson's life.

It had been a long time since Henson was forced to deal with racism on a daily basis. In Greenland, he thought of the Inuit as equals, as they thought of him. In America, he was once again refused entry into buildings and treated with ignorance and sometimes hatred.

It was in the South that he came face to face with this bitter reality. Oranges were thrown at him as he boarded a train. One night, a bullet flew over his head, shattering a window. He witnessed the senseless beating of another porter by a group of white men. He was refused service at

The Pullman Company was hiring only African Americans as porters as late as 1943 when this photograph was taken.

The Pullman Sleeper Cars

A Pullman Palace Car was a luxury railway car that resembled a moving hotel more than an everyday train. It was invented by George Pullman in 1857. These sleeper cars were designed so passengers could ride in comfort and luxury during overnight travel rather than sitting upright in uncomfortable coach seats. The cars were appointed with carpet, plush seating, libraries, barbershops, toilets, and pull-down berths (a type of bunk) with curtains, so passengers could sleep in comfort and privacy. A passenger would book a berth as well as space in the elegant dining car.

The Pullman Company hired African American men as porters to provide personal service for all their passengers. At one time, the company was the largest employer of African Americans in the United States.

The Pullman Company did their best to provide luxurious travel for their clients. As this 1894 advertisement shows, dining cars had linen tablecloths and travelers were served on china.

diners or charged more because the owners did not like the color of his skin. Henson wondered if he was better suited for the harsh climate of the Arctic than the harsh reality of the American South.

After more than two years with the Pullman Company, Henson left his job as a porter and returned to New York City. There he met Lucy Jane Ross at a friend's dinner party. Although she was much younger than Matthew, they fell in love.

Then, while Matthew was working as a janitor, word finally arrived from Peary. They would soon be ready to go again. Although he knew he couldn't say no to this opportunity with Peary, it was going to be hard to leave Lucy behind. Henson knew how difficult spending so much time—possibly years—apart could be on a relationship. He proposed to her anyway and she said yes, under one condition: They would be married when he returned from the North Pole.

A Brand New Ship

During the same period when Henson was working as a porter, Peary was running into difficulties of his own. He found that many people had grown tired of his story. They were losing interest in his quest—and continued failure—to conquer the pole.

Thankfully, Peary still had at least one important supporter— President Theodore Roosevelt, who was enthusiastic about Peary's goal and proud that an American might be the first to the North Pole. Having the president on his side opened

Theodore Roosevelt, the 26th president of the United States (1901–1909) was an enthusiastic supporter of Peary's expeditions. Roosevelt was an outdoorsman, writer, soldier, and winner of the 1906 Nobel Peace Prize.

new doors for Peary. He found new financial backers for yet another expedition.

Peary was fully convinced that his best bet to reach the pole was landing as far north as possible. He had attempted this in 1898 with the *Windward* but was trapped by ice too far south. Peary had learned his lesson. He needed a ship strong enough to break through the ice.

Peary wanted a new ship built to his specific design. Instead of a steel hull, Peary wanted a ship made of wood, which would be more flexible. The hull, or body of the ship, should

Instead of a steel hull, Peary wanted a ship made of wood, which would be more flexible.

also be reinforced with steel beams and rounded on the bottom rather than V-shaped like most other ships that could easily be trapped by ice. A brand new ship, the *Roosevelt*—named after the president for all his support—was built to Peary's specifications.

The hull of the *Roosevelt* was wide and didn't come to a sharp point deep under water. When floes of ice threatened to trap it, the *Roosevelt's* rounded hull could push against the ice and hopefully—thanks to not having the deep bottom of other ships—push its way over it. The weight of the ship would then crush that portion of the floe. In this way, it

The *Roosevelt*—as seen in this undated photograph—was built to withstand the pressure of ice floes and long winters. Peary wanted a tough ship, not necessarily a pretty one.

could slowly make its way through bays, and, hopefully, prevent moving ice from crushing it. Of course, this change wouldn't help in the deep of winter when all the water is frozen solid, but it might get the expedition farther north during the summer months. Peary was proud of his ship and felt confident that it would get him closer to the pole.

Peary hired Robert Bartlett as captain. Bartlett had been an assistant captain on the *Windward* and was a key member of these teams. He was from Newfoundland and a very experienced seaman in the icy waters.

Along with Henson, they would leave New York Harbor in July 1905. Friends, family, and well-wishers, including the president, saw the explorers off at the dock. The *Roosevelt* sailed easily away. Its rounded hull and thick walls ready for the deepest cold of the Arctic.

This 1908 photograph was taken as the *Roosevelt* was about to set sail. President Roosevelt and Peary had great respect for each other and shared a sense of adventure for exploration.

CHAPTER 10

The New Peary System

Had it not been for furious storms enforcing delays and losses of many precious days, the Pole would have been reached.

The *Roosevelt* stopped first at Etah, Greenland, to pick up furs, dogs, and supplies. Henson also encouraged a group of Inuit to come farther north with them. They did, of course, if only because Mahri Pahlak, as the Inuit called Henson, asked them.

The passage to Cape Sheridan on the northern tip of Ellesmere Island—even farther north than Fort Conger—was crowded with ice. The *Roosevelt* pushed its way through under Bartlett's command. It was a slow journey, but by September 5, the ship had arrived. They were still 500 miles from the North Pole, but for the first time, Peary's plan of having a far-north base camp was a reality.

One of the best ways to search for oncoming floes of ice was to stand in the crow's nest. This undated photograph shows Bartlett up high, scanning the waters for dangers.

Two Teams and a Supply Line

One of the most important aspects of The Peary System was his organization of sled teams. Peary had devised a new plan to make it over the great ice. He divided the men into two teams.

The first team was the "pioneer team," and the second team was the "main party." The main party was then broken down into five smaller teams—each made up of one of Peary's men and two Inuit. Each of these three-man teams had their own dogsled team.

The pioneer team would be the first to break a trail over the rough ice.

The smaller three-man teams would then follow the pioneer team, each one leaving a day apart. Peary's three-man team would be the last. In theory, Peary's team should have the easiest time as the trail would be well broken in by then. According to Peary's plan, all of the teams (except the last) would work at setting up the supply line. As each team followed the pioneer team, they would drop off a cache of supplies at designated intervals. At the end of a day, each team would set up a small camp and would build an igloo and leave a cache of supplies for the next team coming along.

The job of the pioneer team was to break a trail over the rough, jagged ice such as the type shown in this undated photograph.

Once a team reached a certain destination point, they would return to the base for more supplies. They would use the igloos and camps already built to rest on their journeys out and back. When the teams were so far out that returning to base camp was inefficient, or impossible, they would return only as far as the last cache for needed supplies.

This method perhaps felt like a lot of backtracking but it was the best way to ensure a constant supply line. In the end, Peary and his team would be the remaining team left to travel to the North Pole. Then, after Peary reached the pole, he could return to the main camp by following the direct line of igloos and caches of food that his teams had established along the way. This should ensure a fast and safe return to land for all the weary travelers.

As practical as The Peary System sounded, Henson later acknowledged there were some problems with it. The teams spent too much time setting up the caches, and the valuable supplies could be wasted because the cairns—or markers for the caches—couldn't always be found. Although the polar ice seemed solid, it drifted—sometimes a fair bit—which made finding the cairns difficult, if not impossible.

Peary understood the difficulties of drifting ice. This is one of the reasons why he moved the base camp a few miles west of Fort Conger to Cape Sheridan. Knowing that the ice drifted east, Peary hoped that by starting slightly west, it would eventually put them perfectly in line with the pole. Unfortunately, it was difficult to say how quickly the ice would move or when it would break up.

Starting Out on the Long March

With their new plan worked out, the Peary expedition started their long march on March 1, 1906. Henson left on the pioneer team. The other teams followed at day intervals as planned, with Peary leaving last on March 6.

Henson and Bartlett took turns breaking the trail for the rest of the teams. Bartlett was a bigger man and stronger, but Henson had much more experience with dog teams. Breaking a trail was very hard work so it was best to share the difficult task. The sleds

An undated photograph shows a man pushing one of Peary's sleds. The long sleds could carry a lot of weight but broke easily on the rough ice.

often broke down with so much weight bouncing on the rough terrain. It was hard on the dogs, the men, and the sleds, and Henson spent a great deal of time fixing, then refixing, the sleds.

The Big Lead

It was still March when Henson was as surprised as the rest of the team by "The Big Lead" they encountered. A lead is a river that flows between two sheets of ice, usually one sheet of ice covers the land and another sheet covers the Polar Sea. One option for a traveler who encounters a lead is to go around it, but that could potentially carry a person too far off course. It was best to wait for the temperature to drop again so a bridge of ice formed over the lead or the floes moved close enough to cross.

On March 26, Henson encountered a lead almost thirty feet wide. He was forced to camp and wait for a bridge of ice to form over it. While he waited, Peary caught up with him. While the other teams went back and forth delivering supplies, Peary had moved quickly along the line. Together, Henson and Peary sat by the lead for a week

Henson was very frustrated. The weather was perfect—they could have made wonderful time across the ice—but the water prevented them from moving.

Sometimes teams used ropes to pull each other from one floe to the next to cross a lead. When the ice was close, the sleds could quickly cross as seen in this undated photograph.

When the teams finally made it across—and Henson again took the pioneer position—they were stopped once more by a severe storm a few days later. Henson was building an igloo to wait it out as Peary's team arrived at his camp. The other teams had still not arrived.

Going Off Course

The winds died down seven days later, and Peary took a navigational reading. They were seventy miles too far east! The wind had blown the drifting ice off course. This was very distressing. It would be hard for the rest of the teams to find them, and they would have difficulty locating the return trail. This meant yet another lost cache of food. They would also have to struggle to make up for lost time and distance. Still, they decided to continue their journey and rushed to get back on track.

Despite being made of snow, igloos were quite warm. Snow was packed tight to keep wind out and the fire heated everything—and everyone—inside. Henson waited out harsh storms in such igloos similar to the one in this modern photograph.

By April 21, they reached a new record of traveling the farthest north. By that time, though, their supplies were running out and it was unsafe to go farther. Once again, they turned back to base. It was difficult for Henson to accept Peary's decision, but he knew the lieutenant was right. They were risking all their lives by continuing. The pole was not to be theirs this time.

After so many tries, Peary was still not successful. They had set a new record for distance, but this was a bittersweet victory. They were so close. Peary and Henson relived the trek over and over. They needed to know what went wrong.

There was also the added burden of age. Peary was fifty years old and Henson was forty. Peary still had trouble with his feet after losing his toes and often had to ride on a sled rather than walk. Quite likely, they had only one more chance. They would have to convince investors that two older men were physically capable of completing the mission. They would have to hope that after so many years and so much strain and struggle, they would have the strength.

Mrs. Peary's Fund-raising Efforts

All the while that Henson and Peary were north trying to reach the pole, Peary's wife, Josephine, was trying to raise more money. She wanted her husband home safe but knew he wouldn't rest until he reached the North Pole. These ventures were expensive, so Mrs. Peary sought out investors to support them.

Morris K. Jessup was a key supporter of Peary and his expeditions. Unfortunately, Jessup, who died in 1906, did not live long enough to see the outcome of Peary's expedition.

Mrs. Peary was tireless in contacting museums, politicians, and wealthy members of society, especially in New York City and Washington, D.C. She gave interviews and published her own journals of her arctic adventures. Mrs. Peary was almost as well known as her husband. She helped secure one of Peary's most generous supporters, Morris K. Jessup, the president of the Museum of Natural History. Peary's last two expeditions on the *Roosevelt* might not have happened without Jessup's support.

Returning Home Again

The *Roosevelt* arrived back in New York City on Christmas Eve 1906. It was slow-going getting back as the ship was trapped in ice several times. Henson was frustrated by all the delays and anxious to return home. He wanted to see Lucy. This was the first time that he felt he was heading home to something, rather than leaving everything behind.

Peary asked Henson to stay with the ship while it sat in the dock. The *Roosevelt* was in serious need of repair. It had done well against all that ice, but the ice had taken its toll. Peary paid Henson $25 per month to stay on board and oversee all the repairs. The repairs took much longer than expected, and he was there until the summer. Even so, Matthew still found time to see his beloved Lucy.

Peary's backers were heartened by the lieutenant's success. Landing so far north appeared to be the answer. President Roosevelt, in particular, felt that their next venture would be the successful one—so much so that he appointed Peary to the position of commander in the U.S. Navy.

Peary retired from the navy in 1911 with the rank of rear admiral. The navy paid tribute to Peary by naming several ships after him.

Finally, all the repairs were done and the date for their next departure was set—July 1908. To celebrate, Matthew married Lucy Ross in the fall of 1907. With that, everything was set for what would be—successful or not—their last attempt to reach the North Pole.

CHAPTER 11

One Last Chance to Reach the Pole

We will plant the Stars and Stripes—at the North Pole!
—Robert E. Peary

An excited, boisterous crowd gathered on the dock at New York City Harbor to see the new Peary expedition off on July 6, 1908. While this new expedition had the backing of the president and the American Museum of Natural History, not everyone supported it. Some newspapers argued that too much time and money had been wasted on Peary's folly. They did not feel as confident as Peary and the president that this trip would be successful.

As always, Henson watched from the deck. He was happy to be on his way but felt tired just thinking of what lay ahead. He knew this would be his last trip north. He was beginning to wonder if he was too old for this type of work. He had a mix of emotions. There was his life's work in the Arctic and there was his life at home with a new bride waiting for his return.

A faded 1906 photograph of Henson was taken onboard the *Roosevelt* while in Sydney, Nova Scotia. Henson is pictured with dogs and snowshoes.

Crew of the 1908 Expedition

For the 1908 expedition, Robert Bartlett returned to the North as captain of the *Roosevelt*. He would also rejoin the team crossing the ice cap to the North Pole. After his adventures on the ice in 1905 and 1906, Bartlett was an experienced sled driver. Ross G. Marvin, an engineer, also joined the team.

The remaining crew was made up of John W. Goodsell, the team's physician, George Borup, a twenty-one-year-old graduate from Yale University, and Donald B. MacMillan, an engineer and university professor, who returned to the Arctic many times after his trek with Peary and wrote a dictionary of the Inuit language.

Henson (far right) sits with other members of the crew on one of the sleds that went to the North Pole. This 1909 photo was taken onboard the *Roosevelt* on their journey home.

Peary was anxious throughout the journey. There were other explorers vying for the pole, including Dr. Cook, the same man who had accompanied Peary on his first expedition to Greenland. Cook had set out in the fall of 1907 and was already in the North. Peary felt sure that Cook had assembled an expedition to get to the pole first, and he considered this the ultimate betrayal from a former teammate.

A 1908 photograph shows Dr. Cook in arctic furs and holding pen and paper.
He wrote several popular books about his arctic adventures.

Preparing for the Final Trek

The *Roosevelt* landed at Cape Sheridan on September 5,
1908. The crew quickly began the task of setting up the ship for
winter. Peary had a comfortable stateroom for himself that
included a piano and library. The rest of the men stayed in a
common area with a few personal items that they brought north.
Henson brought only books—a novel by Charles Dickens and
the Bible. Some of the Inuit families—this time most were
recruited from the Cape York settlement—stayed on board, but
many set up igloos or tents nearby.

Throughout the fall, the team alternated between hunting
trips and taking supplies ninety-three miles northeast to Cape
Columbia. There always seemed to be something more to do and
Henson always kept busy. As MacMillan said, "A carpenter, he

built the sledges [sleds], a mechanic, he made the alcohol stoves, an expert dog driver, he taught us to handle our dogs. Highly respected by the Eskimos, he was easily the most popular man on board ship."

Despite the darkening days and dropping temperatures, time passed quickly. The men had musical instruments and a phonograph for entertainment. They celebrated Christmas with

The *Roosevelt* was a more comfortable winter home than living in a tent or igloo. This c. 1908 photograph shows the ship wintering at Cape Sheridan.

champagne and mincemeat pies, and Henson fired three shots into the air on December 22 to announce the return of the sun. They were in good spirits and ready for their long march.

During the summer months, as seen in this 1909 photograph, the men moved some of their supplies from the *Roosevelt* onto land.

Getting Under Way

On February 18, 1909, Henson left the *Roosevelt*, perhaps for the last time. They would use the same system—a pioneer team followed by the main party—as they did in 1906. Peary and his Inuit companions would leave last and conserve their energy for the final run to the pole.

Henson was trekking with three Inuit, four sleds, and twenty-four dogs. Their sleds, weighing approximately 250 pounds each, were loaded down with pemmican, condensed milk, and alcohol for the stoves. They were following the trail already pioneered by Bartlett and George Borup, the young man from Yale University. Henson and his companions arrived in Cape Columbia on February 22. It was their farthest north camp but still 413 miles from the pole.

Unlike with their other settlements, the team did not spend time setting up the structures above at Cape Columbia. It was to be a very temporary home before they headed north to the pole.

The next few days were spent readying the sleds and waiting for all the teams to arrive. Then on February 28, 1909, Peary sent Bartlett out to start breaking the trail, followed by Henson and his men a day later.

Henson still had to use his pickaxe to get over the ice despite following the already broken trail. The heavily loaded sleds tipped easily as they banged along the rough parts. Henson was only an hour or two from camp when one of his sleds broke down. He fixed it as quickly as possible but was hampered by the cold. Henson followed one of the Inuit tricks of warming his hands under his shirt to prevent frostbite. Soon he was back on the trail, following Bartlett's team.

Held Up by a Lead

On their second day, they were stopped by a lead. Henson and his team walked west until they found ice to cross over it. Their good fortune ended quickly, though, as they found a second lead only a few miles away. While they waited, Peary's and MacMillan's teams caught up with them.

Because of Commander Peary's prior foot injury, he was forced to ride on a sled most of the way with his Inuit aides walking or driving the team.

The men spent another six days waiting by the lead, consuming precious supplies and feeling frustrated.They tried to amuse themselves with songs and Inuit games. They stomped their feet to keep the blood circulating, and hopefully, prevent frostbite. Everyone was nervous and concerned but did their best to hide it from each other. When a bridge of ice finally formed, they all rushed across it and continued on their way.

Preparing for the Last Leg

Everyone on the expedition knew that only one of them would accompany Peary on the final leg. No one knew whom he would pick or when the rest of them might be sent back. The commander planned to make his decision as they traveled north. He couldn't predict who might be injured or too tired. Starting at 300 miles from the pole, he sent them back one team at a time. The first to go was MacMillan and Dr. Goodsell, then Borup, and then Marvin. Finally, there were only Bartlett and Henson left.

Robert Bartlett (1875–1946)

This undated photograph shows Robert Bartlett aboard the *Roosevelt*.

An accomplished sea captain, Robert Bartlett went north with Peary three times and in 1909 was awarded the Hubbard Medal, the National Geographic Society's highest honor, for his efforts with Peary in the Arctic. Bartlett, an Inuit of Newfoundland, came from a family of sailors. He was working on ships while still a teenager and eventually piloted more than forty expeditions into arctic waters.

In 1913, he piloted the *Karluk* into the Canadian Arctic. He is credited with saving the lives of its crew when the ship was trapped by ice. Vilhjalmur Stefansson, the expedition leader, abandoned the ship to continue his trek through the Arctic. When Bartlett realized that a rescue ship would not arrive, he walked 700 miles over ice to Siberia and brought back a rescue party.

Bartlett died in New York City in 1946 and is buried in his hometown of Brigus, Newfoundland.

Bartlett was a valuable team member. Not only had he captained a ship through icy waters on several expeditions, but he also took on the very difficult task of breaking the trail over land and ice. Peary was certain Bartlett was strong enough to go the final distance, but he based his decision on other factors.

Henson had been with Peary on all his arctic journeys but one. This type of loyalty meant a great deal to Peary. It was also important that Henson was very skilled at driving his team over the ice. "He could handle dogs and sledges [sleds]. He was a part of the traveling machine." As Peary later wrote, "He was the best man I had with me for this kind of work."

On April 1, 1909, Bartlett was sent back. Before leaving, Peary allowed Bartlett to take his sled farther north—approximately 133 miles from the pole—so Bartlett could set a new record for farthest north. Before Bartlett headed south again, he shook each of their hands and gave a cheery good-bye.

This photograph was taken of Bartlett just before he turned back to camp in April 1909.

There were now six men left. Peary, Henson, and their four Inuit companions, Ootah, Ooqueah, Egingwah, and Seegloo, were ready for the final stretch. With Bartlett gone, Henson and his team broke the trail most of the way. Peary, riding on the sled, followed with his team. They still had more than a hundred miles to go.

On April 3, Henson suffered a terrible scare. Sometimes the teams could feel the sea moving below them and the ice itself moving as they marched across it. Henson was following the rest of the team, pushing his sled over a tough patch, when his foot slipped and he fell into the water.

In only a matter of seconds, Ootah grabbed Henson and pulled him out. Henson barely had time to register that he was in the water before his good friend hauled him back onto the ice. Ootah had saved Henson's life and brought his sled and dogs to safety.

Henson checked the contents of the sled. He was carrying the navigational and scientific equipment and relaxed when he saw all was well. The water on his coat and hood immediately turned to ice. Henson beat himself to knock the ice crystals off and changed into a dry pair of boots. It had all happened so quickly, and then they were on the march again with hardly a pause.

The Big Day Finally Arrives

In early evening of April 5, 1909, Peary took a navigational reading and discovered they were thirty-five miles from the pole. Peary ordered them to make camp so they could get some well-deserved rest.

Henson couldn't sleep, though. He didn't want to get overconfident—so many things could happen in those last miles. Peary must have felt the same because he was soon up and loading his sled. They were back on the trail by midnight.

Around noon the next day, April 6, they stopped once more. Henson and the Inuit men built igloos while Peary organized the equipment. When Henson noticed Peary unfolding his American flag, he suspected they had reached their destination. He watched as Peary took his sextant and compass and started to take his readings.

With Henson watching him, Commander Peary reported that they were less than five miles from the pole. Considering the nature of the North Pole—that shifting ice over the Polar Sea makes it difficult to maintain any position for long—Peary was satisfied that they had arrived! Their achievement would certainly stand in the history books. When Peary announced that they should "plant the Stars and Stripes at the North Pole," Henson let out a cheer. Peary named their site Camp Morris Jessup in honor of the benefactor from the Museum of Natural History.

With the flag waving behind them, Henson tried to shake Peary's hand, but the commander turned away. At first, Henson suspected that the wind or some dust got in Peary's eyes—that he was weary and needed to rest—and that he didn't see Henson's extended hand. However, the commander's later actions would indicate that there might have been more to it.

Peary took this photograph when he reached the North Pole. Henson and the four Inuit men stand in front of the flag that Josephine Peary had made for her husband.

The entire party retreated to their igloos for rest. When Henson awoke, Peary was gone. He and two Inuit men had left camp to take more readings. Peary returned and announced that he had in fact gone past the pole. He was at last satisfied that Camp Jessup would mark "the top of the world."

Peary and Henson took turns photographing the team beneath the American flag.

The Americans looked tired and elated while the Inuit looked confused by all the fuss. They could see no difference between this ice and the ice close to home.

After thirty hours at Camp Jessup, the team reloaded their sleds and started back. For perhaps the first time, they met with few mishaps on their journey. They returned along the same trail so most of the way was broken in. There were no major storms or high winds and even the leads were manageable. They were back on the *Roosevelt* on April 26, 1909.

After going off course, Henson and Peary reached the farthest north in 1906. All of Peary's previous expeditions are shown on this map, starting with the 1892 expedition to Independence Bay and finally ending at the North Pole in 1909.

CHAPTER 12

Returning Home

The Pole at last!!! The prize of three centuries, my dream and ambition for twenty-three years. Mine at last.

—*Robert E. Peary*

Upon returning to the *Roosevelt*, Henson's and Peary's excitement was soon shattered by the news that Ross Marvin did not return. Apparently, he fell through the ice at one of the leads and his Inuit companions couldn't save him. Henson was deeply saddened by this news. He was fond of Marvin and considered him a friend.

It was now time to say good-bye. It was with mixed emotions that Henson shook the hands of the Inuit who saw them off. Henson was excited about going home. He wanted to see Lucy and start a life with her. However, Henson also knew that he would not be back in Greenland. Saying good-bye to his Inuit friends meant he wouldn't see them again. Henson wished them well, saying he would never forget them, and followed Peary onto the ship. The *Roosevelt* stopped in England so the men could send telegrams home, including one to Peary's wife Josephine: "The Pole at last!!! The prize of three centuries, my dream and ambition for twenty-three years. Mine at last." After decades of hard work and so much sacrifice, they were finally returning as heroes.

The Heroes Return

Henson walked off the *Roosevelt* and onto the dock. It was a shock being back in civilization. Even though New York City was his home, it always took time to readjust. The sights and sounds of city life, the buildings, people, carriages, and smells, were the opposite of life he had just returned from. He was anxious to see his wife, and he wanted to take advantage of his success and start a new career. Henson was now forty-three years old, and he knew there would be no more expeditions to the North.

The newspapers were filled with stories of their triumph. Of course, the papers considered it Peary's success. Henson was barely mentioned. He was described as Commander Peary's "negro assistant" or his "black manservant." They never called him an explorer.

Prejudice was not new to him, but Henson had hoped attitudes would be different this time. He had accomplished something great, after all. It was something that no one—no matter what his or her color—had done before.

Reporters quickly surrounded him, rapidly asking questions, wanting details about the trek. He

The front page from this September 9, 1909, issue of the *New York Times* announces Robert Peary's triumphant journey to the North Pole. Matthew Henson was disappointed that the newspapers did not give him credit for successfully reaching the pole as well.

On March 5, 1910, a dinner was held at the Hotel Astor in New York to honor Peary. Henson was not invited to the dinner.

expected them to ask about his life, his experiences in the North, and what he planned to do next. Instead, most of their questions were about Dr. Frederick Cook, who claimed that he had reached the pole first. They wanted to know Henson's thoughts on the controversy.

Henson was surprised that Cook's claim was taken seriously. He answered all the reporters questions, saying he doubted Cook reached the pole, and explaining why Peary's claim was valid. Henson had interviewed the Inuit who traveled with Cook, and according to them, Cook did not get that far north.

Henson liked being the center of attention, to have so many people seek out his opinion. He felt like all his hard work would finally be recognized. He was certain that a life of fame lay before him.

He was wrong, though. Fame would not come to Henson, not for many years.

Not the Welcome He Expected

Matthew Henson was not recognized by members of the explorer or scientific communities. When the National

Dr. Frederick A. Cook (1865–1940)

When Peary and Henson returned from the North Pole in 1909, they learned that Dr. Cook was claiming he reached the pole in April 1908, a full year before Peary. This controversy caused a huge stir at the time, and even though Peary has since been credited as the first man to the pole, the debate still continues.

The scientific community and geographic societies pored over Peary's notes and questioned whether he would have been able to reach the pole and return in such a short time. Cook's claim was more difficult to prove as his navigational records and diaries were lost in the North. Although he was attacked in the press at the time—attacks often led by Peary's camp—Cook still had a number of supporters, including fellow explorers Roald Amundsen and Adolphus Greely. In truth, there are many who still believe Cook was cheated out of his rightful title of first man at the North Pole,

This wasn't Cook's only controversy. In 1906, he claimed to be the first man to reach the summit of Mount McKinley. This claim was later discredited when his photographs were proven to be forgeries. Cook spent his later years defending his claim with little success.

The Peary/Cook controversy was discussed worldwide. It even appeared on the cover of a magazine from Paris in 1909.

Upon returning from the North Pole, the National Geographic Society issued a special medal to Peary. It is dated December 15, 1909.

Geographic Society awarded Peary their highest award—the Hubbard Medal—in 1906 for retrieving the meteorites and mapping Northern Greenland, Henson was not mentioned. In 1909, after their last successful trip north, the society awarded the Hubbard Medal to Robert Bartlett, the captain of the *Roosevelt,* but Henson was again ignored. He was not admitted to the Explorer's Club of New York or acknowledged as an equal by its members.

Only the black community celebrated his great achievements. Dinners were given in his honor, and he received special gifts. Henson was an inspiration for those who struggled to achieve their goals despite prejudices. However, the early 1900s was a time when race, too often, determined a person's success.

Henson hoped his journey to the pole would help him start a new career. He had accomplished a seemingly impossible task, and he was excited about his place in the history books. Perhaps he could make his living as a speaker. At the very least, he could enjoy some time in the spotlight. Henson made several attempts to build upon his success, but he ran into several roadblocks. The first and the biggest obstacle was Peary.

CHAPTER 13

A Slow but Sure Legacy

From the time we knew we were at the Pole,
Commander Peary scarcely spoke to me. . . .
I thought this over and it grieved me very much.

Henson quickly realized Peary wanted nothing to do him after the discovery of the pole. "From the time we knew we were at the Pole, Commander Peary scarcely spoke to me. . . . I thought this over and over and it grieved me very much."

It could have been that Peary was simply done with Henson, who had served his purpose in getting Peary to the pole and nothing more was required. They lived in completely different social and economic circles. Perhaps Peary thought of them as strictly boss and employee and saw no reason for further contact.

There is also the theory that Henson, as the driver of the lead sled team, was actually the first to arrive at the North Pole. Henson believed this was the cause of the split. He claimed that Peary intended to go ahead on his own but

A 1909 photograph shows Peary on the deck of the *Roosevelt*. He is wearing his full arctic costume. Soon after reaching the pole, Henson noticed a change in Peary's attitude toward him.

miscalculated the distance because he was riding in a sled rather than walking. As years passed, as it often seemed to happen with Henson's stories, the time that he waited at the pole for Peary to arrive became longer and longer. Eventually, Henson claimed he had waited so long that he had time to build an igloo and make tea before the commander's arrival.

There is also the matter of Peary having to ride on the sled for most of the way. He was a proud man and this might have been humiliating. He might have hoped to keep that part of the story a secret.

These questions will never be answered with satisfaction, though. Following their return from the pole, there was very little contact between the two men. Although Peary did extend some courtesies to Henson later on, the commander rarely spoke of Henson.

Harsh Restrictions

Every member of Peary's team—including Henson—had to sign an oath of loyalty. They were not allowed to publish anything or provide information for a publication until one year after Peary's book appeared. He also demanded that all diaries and photographs be turned over to him. Any attempt at earning a living by discussing or telling any of these experiences must be approved by Peary.

Every member of Peary's team—including Henson—had to sign an oath of loyalty.

One of the first things that Henson did upon his return was go on a lecture tour. Peary's tour of 1893 was very successful, so Henson expected something similar. Henson contacted Peary about using his own photographs from Camp Jessup. Henson assumed that because he used his own camera and he had paid for the film and the processing, that he should be allowed use of them. Peary refused.

The situation escalated from there. Henson went on tour anyway, using photos that he still had, and Peary sent angry telegrams trying to put a stop to it. Henson pointed out that he wasn't getting any younger and had a wife to support. This was a chance for him to earn some money. He also reminded Peary that he had been paid very little for all his years of dedication.

The argument was somewhat pointless, though. Henson's lecture tour was a failure. He was uncomfortable in the spotlight and giving a prepared speech. There was also the problem of tickets sales. People simply weren't buying tickets to see Henson, so the tour was cut short. "He was an intelligent, good-looking, soft-spoken, dead-panned, modest fellow," tour organizer William Brady said. "I was sure he would easily ingratiate himself with audiences. A set-up—but it didn't work."

If Peary heard any of the content of Henson's talks, he would have been relieved that the tour was cancelled. This was when Henson originally made the claim that he was the first to the pole and that Peary was pulled almost the entire way on a sled.

Henson's Published Account

After the publication of Robert Peary's book *The North Pole*, Henson signed a book contract for his own story. Peary was uncomfortable with Henson producing a book. They came to an agreement that Peary would have final say on the edits. If there were anything he didn't like, then the publisher would change it.

To show his good will, though, Peary wrote an introduction to the book. He focused less on Henson's skill as an explorer and more on his race. According to Peary, it was remarkable that a black man could survive in the Arctic. Peary doesn't mention that

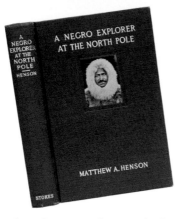

A first edition copy of Henson's book *A Negro Explorer at the North Pole*. The book was first published in 1911.

without Henson's skill and assistance, he never would have made it to the pole.

Henson's book *A Negro Explorer at the North Pole* was published in 1912. Despite Henson's hopes of success and royalties, not many copies were sold. Henson was starting to realize that recognition might never come.

Matthew and Lucy were struggling for money. They both wanted to stay in New York but Henson would have to find work. He thought back to the time in 1891 when he had to choose between working with the navy and going north. Henson thought Peary would always take care of him if he remained loyal. He tried once more to contact Peary and ask for help.

Finally Getting Recognized

In 1913, Peary relented. He arranged for Henson to take a job at the U.S. Customs House in New York City as a messenger. Henson stayed at this job until his retirement in 1936. He gave the occasional interview and lecture, but his name largely disappeared from the public's awareness. He might

Henson poses for a photograph c. 1926 while working at the U.S. Customs House in New York City.

Henson poses for a photograph c. 1948 as he receives an Honorary
Member status—one of the highest honors—from the Explorers Club.

have continued this quiet existence were it not for his few
supporters who continued to champion his cause.

Two explorers, Peter Freuchen of Norway and Vilhjalmur
Stefansson of Canada, did not let the subject rest until Henson
was accepted into the Explorer's Club—the prestigious club for
famous explorers and scientists. That finally happened in 1937.
Today, the Explorer's Club in New York City proudly displays
Henson's sled from the final trek.

Slowly but surely, Henson started to receive awards proving
that he wasn't completely forgotten. In 1944, the U.S. Congress
created a special medal called the Peary Polar Medal. It was
awarded to all the members of the *Roosevelt* party who went
north in 1908, including Henson.

The Explorer's Club

Founded in 1904, the club was a meeting place for explorers and scientists. It provided funding, grants, and support for expeditions and projects to remote and unexplored areas of the world. Its members were the first to reach the North and South Poles, the moon, and the deepest trench in the ocean. Aldophus Greely was its first president. Robert Peary and Dr. Frederick Cook both held that position in subsequent years.

The Explorer's Club continues to support expeditions and adventurers all over the world through its various offices. It also gives an annual dinner to celebrate that year's achievements in exploration and offers awards for oceanography and mountain climbing, among others. Today, many of these projects focus on environmental issues rather than on exploration.

Then in 1947, *Dark Companion* was published. Although the author, Bradley Robinson, collaborated closely with Henson, it's hard to say how much of the book is true. The book reads more like an adventure novel than a historical nonfiction narrative or biography. It did, however, bring Henson into the public limelight. *Dark Companion* was a popular book, and more people became aware of Henson's life and accomplishments.

In 1954, President Dwight D. Eisenhower received Matthew and Lucy Henson at the White House to celebrate the anniversary of reaching the pole. Henson received a presidential citation for his work in the Arctic. Their picture was taken beside a globe with Henson's hand pointing to the very place, right at the top of the world, where he once stood.

Henson and Lucy visit with President Eisenhower at the White House in 1954. This photograph marks the 45th anniversary of Henson reaching the pole.

Henson died in New York City on March 9, 1955. He and Lucy had so little money that she couldn't afford a proper funeral befitting a man of his accomplishments. Instead, he was simply buried in a grave next to Lucy's mother in a New York cemetery.

Matthew Henson's Legacy

Henson's story does not end with his death. He found more fame after he died than he had ever enjoyed while alive. During the 1960s and 1970s and the rise of the civil rights movement and African American studies in colleges, Henson gained more supporters.

A plaque was erected in his honor at the Maryland Statehouse in 1961. Then in 1988, thanks to the efforts of Professor Allen Counter of Harvard University, Matthew and Lucy's graves were moved from Brooklyn to Arlington Cemetery, just outside of Washington, D.C. They were reburied next to Peary. After that, a U.S. Navy survey ship was named the *Matthew Henson* in 1996.

Although Lucy and Matthew had no children together, Henson did father a son in the Arctic, and some of his descendants from Greenland came for the ceremony. They

stood proudly by his grave while Henson was finally honored by his country for his contribution to the world of exploration.

Henson continued to receive honors and tributes. In 1986, the U.S. Postal Service released a stamp honoring Peary and Henson to celebrate their work in the Arctic. The Matthew Henson Earth Conservation Center, sponsored by the Earth Conservation Corps in Washington, D.C., opened in 2002. It is dedicated to preserving wildlife and plants along the Anacostia River in Maryland near Washington, D.C.

Anaukkaq Henson, Matthew's Inuit son, traveled from Greenland to attend his father's reburial in Arlington National Cemetery in 1988.

In 2000, the National Geographic Society awarded him the Hubbard Medal posthumously. Almost a hundred years earlier, they had passed him over and given the medal to Robert Bartlett. This was the first time that the society awarded the Hubbard Medal to someone after their death. At long last, they were righting an their old wrong. Matthew Henson, explorer, was once again at the top of the world.

Matthew Henson is shown in an undated photograph as he will always be remembered. He is wearing his arctic clothing and looking into the distance.

In 1986, the U.S. Postage Service issued a stamp to honor Peary and Henson.

Glossary

American Museum of Natural History—a museum in New York City that houses thousands of specimens of animals, fish, plants, and artifacts of cultural groups around the world.

axis—an imaginary line that cuts through the center of the planet from north to south about which the earth spins. The North Pole is the north end of the axis.

BCE—Before Common Era: any year that occurs before year 0. For example, 326 BCE is 326 years before year 0, which marks the start of the Common Era.

CE—Common Era: any year that occurs after year 0. For example, Matthew Henson was born in 1866 CE.

Civil War (1861–1865)—the war between the Northern and Southern states that ultimately ended slavery in America.

dehydration—lacking the necessary amount of water in the body.

equator—an imaginary geographical line that cuts across the center of the earth and is equal distance from both the North and the South pole.

frostbite—damage to skin caused by extreme cold. Fingers, toes, and noses are most often affected.

ice cap—a permanent sheet of ice that covers the land of northern Greenland.

meteorites—meteors, which are large rocks or pieces of metal, usually iron, that land on Earth from outer space.

Northwest Passage—a sailing lane through the islands in Canada's north, used primarily as a trade route.

prejudice—having preconceived feelings of hatred or dislike toward other races, sexes, or religious groups without basis or reason.

racism—believing that one's race determines intelligence, cultural, or social standing and that one race is more important and powerful than others.

red lichen—a red-colored, moss-like fungus that grows on rocks and trees.

segregation—the separation of the races so that areas, buildings, or community organizations were either white or African American only.

sextant—a navigational instrument that measures longitude and latitude based on the sun's position against the horizon.

snowshoes—wide, flat, webbed shoes that enable their wearer to walk on snow without sinking into it.

survey—to measure land and determine boundaries of a certain area, most often used when mapping an area for construction.

walrus blubber—the fat layer on a walrus that serves as both food and fuel to the people of the North.

young ice—newly formed ice that is often quite thin.

Bibliography

Books

Angell, Pauline K. *To the Top of the World*. New York: Rand McNally & Company, 1964.

Berton, Pierre. *The Arctic Grail*. Toronto: Anchor Books, 2001.

Borup, George. *A Tenderfoot with Peary*. New York: Frederick A. Stokes Company, 1911.

Bramwell, Martyn. *Polar Exploration: Journeys to the Arctic and Antarctic*. Toronto: Stoddart Publishing Co., 1999.

Bryce, Robert M. *Cook & Peary: the Polar Controversy Resolved*. Mechanicsburg: Stackpole Books, 1997.

Counter, S. Allen. *North Pole Legacy: Black, White & Eskimo*. Amherst: University of Massachusetts Press, 1991

Freuchen, Peter. *Adventures in the Arctic*. New York: Julian Messner, Inc., 1960.

Henson, Matthew. *A Negro Explorer at the North Pole*. New York: Cooper Square Press, 2001.

Mowat, Farley. *Polar Passion*. Toronto: McLelland & Stewart, 1967.

Peary, Robert E. *The North Pole*. Toronto: The Copp, Clark Co., 1910.

Robinson, Bradley, in collaboration with Henson, Matthew. *Dark Companion*. New York: Fawcett Premier Edition, 1967.

Stefansson, Vilhjalmur. *Great Adventures and Explorations*. New York: The Dial Press, 1947.

Weems, John Edward. Peary: *The Explorer and the Man*. Boston: Houghton Mifflin Company, 1967.

Periodicals

Ayres Jr., B. Drummond, "Matt Henson, Aide to Pole, Rejoins Pole" *New York Times,* April 7, 1988.

Boston American, interview from July 17, 1910.

Source Notes

The following citations list the sources of quoted material in this book. The first and last few words of each quotation are cited and followed by their source. Complete information on referenced sources can be found in the Bibliography.

Abbreviations used:
BA—Boston American interview
DC—Dark Companion
NE—A Negro Explorer at the North Pole
NP—The North Pole
NYT—New York Times article

INTRODUCTION: To Reach the North Pole
PAGE 1 *"Henson must...without him"*: NYT, April 7,1988

CHAPTER 1: Henson's Story Begins
PAGE 2 *"Your fight...your fists, Matthew."*: DC, p. 38
PAGE 9 *"Your life...with your fists."*: DC, p. 38
PAGE 9 *"Your fight...and intelligence."*: DC, p. 38
PAGE 9 *"These books...your fists, Matthew."*: DC, p. 38

CHAPTER 2: A New Adventure in Nicaragua
PAGE 11 *"It is well...his success."*: NE, p. 11

CHAPTER 3: The North Greenland Expedition
PAGE 18 *"Naturally the...life meant."*: NE, p. 6
PAGE 28 *"Never before...me deeply."*: NE, p.29
PAGE 33 *"Unlike many...as an inferior."*: DC, p.9

CHAPTER 4: The Trek Begins
PAGE 34 *"When I...warmer lands."*: NE, p. 10
PAGE 38 *"I have...these people."*: NE, p. 7
PAGE 38 *"I know every...me as theirs."*: NE, p. 7
PAGE 42 *"with the...warmer lands."*: NE, p. 10

CHAPTER 5: A Second Expedition to Greenland
PAGE 44 *"From now on...to imagine."*: NE, p. 76

CHAPTER 6: Difficult Years in the North
PAGE 53 *"...The recollections...most vivid."*: NE, p. 9
PAGE 53 *"Henson, with...an Eskimo."*: NP, p. 272

Image Credits

About the

Kathleen Olms   She has written abridged
versions of class   ot cards, and more than a few
poems. She lives   which is still far below the land of ice
and snow.

Index